Publishing Online for Writers

Lisa Kesteven

Publishing Online for Writers

palgrave
macmillan

Lisa Kesteven
National Association of Writers in Education
London, UK

ISBN 978-3-031-21365-6   ISBN 978-3-031-21366-3   (eBook)
https://doi.org/10.1007/978-3-031-21366-3

This Palgrave Macmillan imprint is published by the registered company Springer Nature Switzerland AG
The registered company address is: Gewerbestrasse 11, 6330 Cham, Switzerland

I would like to dedicate this book to:
Sebastiaan and Samantha

Contents

I Publishing Online for Writers

II   Publishing E-books

III   Publishing Online: Making It a Success

Publishing Online for Writers

Contents

Introduction to Publishing Online for Writers

Contents

© The Author(s), under exclusive license to Springer Nature Switzerland AG 2023
L. Kesteven, *Publishing Online for Writers*,
https://doi.org/10.1007/978-3-031-21366-3_1

About this Chapter

In this chapter we will:
- Understand how publishing online has developed over the past 50 years and its place in the overall publishing world
- Consider the many and varied ways writers and readers interact with digital platforms
- Understand the difference between an indie author and a self-published author
- Good reasons to have a digital presence and publish online (and when not to)
- EXERCISE: Research about Writing Online
- CHECKLIST: Publishing Online

To begin though, let's be honest—there is something magical about holding a book in your hand, especially a new one that has been freshly printed. The smell of the paper, the touch of the crisp sheets, such a treat! Likewise with magazines and their glossy pages, such enticing use of images, and dynamic colours. But, I bet you are thinking right now: Why is the author of a textbook about publishing online opening with a line like that? Well, stay with me.

I recently learned that such physical pleasures come at a big cost. I was faced with the daunting task of downsizing my library, and I could no longer keep all those bookshelves and bookshelves stacked with books (some two rows deep). Meanwhile my Kindle sat on my desk, alongside my smartphone; I could almost sense they were mocking me. If only I'd bought those books digitally, I reflected, I could have kept them all. Interestingly too, I discovered books hidden in the shadowy depths of my bookshelves that I'd long forgotten about. If I'd had them on my e-book reader, I could have used the search facility and easily browsed through my collection. Not to mention the simple fact that I could have taken them all with me on those long train journeys and holidays. Hundreds of books, an entire library, tucked into my bag with no excess baggage weight to carry.

Will Online Publishing Rid the World of Printed Publications?

It's an interesting question which has been around for a long time. Perhaps some time in the future it might, but I expect it is some time away yet. Despite the increasing popularity of reading online, we still have bookstores (thankfully) and people do still want to browse (which I love to do) and buy physical books—and there are always good reasons to do so. The number of books that end up in charity shops and book stalls at fairs is a testament to this—but if you are as voracious reader as I am, there are natural constraints.

Let us not forget, there is a huge history in literary and print culture. The tactile nature of reading, curling up with a good book, settling down with a novel or a collection of poetry, or even sitting down with a daily newspaper, has been with us for centuries. In 1439, Johannes Gutenberg was the first European to develop a process for mass-producing movable type; the use of oil-based ink for printing books, and most importantly inventing a wooden printing press for the mass production of books. Prior to this, books were handwritten, hand illustrated and physically handmade. Early in the fifteenth century, the book trade was born, and millions of books have since emerged. Think of the titles to hit the shelves since then. Controversially, *The Bible* and D. H. Lawrence's *Lady Chatterley's Lover*, Dante's epic poem, *La commedia*, later named *La divina commedia* (*The Divine Comedy*), *The Ingenious Gentleman Don Quixote of la Mancha Novel* by Miguel de Cervantes, considered by some to be the first novel ever published, through to J. K. Rowling's eponymous Harry Potter series which has sold more than 500 million copies worldwide. And then there are chapbooks, self-help books, non-fiction, academic books, poetry books, and so on; the list being endless and an ongoing project. I wonder, if we could pile them all up, would we be able to reach the moon? If Earth to the Moon is 15,134,310,000 inches and if we take each book as an inch, actually we have about 15 billion books still to go (estimated published books is 129,864,880—great resource the internet, isn't it).

Fast forward from 1439 to 1971, Project Gutenberg, a volunteer project to digitise out-of-copyright books, was born. As a result, we can have free access to some of the most amazing books ever. Type 'Dickens Gutenberg' into Google and take a look, or Bronte or Austen. You will never have time to read them all, yet what a resource! Today, Project Gutenberg has over 75,000 items in its collection, with an average of over 50 new e-books being added each week.

What is clear is that the book industry, and with it the publishing industry, has changed hugely since 1439. The electronic text entails many, many more opportunities to publish. And yet, to some extent, the attitude to publishing is very similar to how it has always been. All of us, as writers, want to see our work in print and for readers everywhere to be able to access. Take Charles Dickens' *A Christmas Carol*. Chapman and Hall, his publishers, did not support the project at all and considered it strange. Consequently, they refused to pay the full costs for publishing it, so Dickens had paid the remainder himself. Who would have thought it, Charles Dickens, world famous author, had to finance the publication of what went on to become his biggest ever seller, never having been out of print since that first edition in 1843 (which you can now read for free). Another fast forward brings us to today, and the knowledge that we too can publish, as Dickens did. In fact, it is easier for us, as this book will go on to explain.

Let's face it, having things digital is a huge space saver. Remember those shelves of CDs (and perhaps for some, those shelves of records)? They quickly became a relic of the past with the advent of music streaming services. Likewise, with magazines and journals—most of which are printed in colour on glossy paper. And it is not just our cluttered homes that are paying the price. If there was ever a burning (literally) reason to go paperless, then surely our planet and climate change is precisely that. Clearly this is where publishing online has a benefit over traditional printing. Fewer trees are cut down and the distribution impact is minimal.

So, How Big Is the Move to Publishing Online?

Let's look at some of the basic facts:

We Are Social (► https://wearesocial.com) call themselves a global socially led creative agency with unrivalled social media expertise. Okay, that sounds like marketing spiel but I found out about them for a very good reason: Each year they publish a number of reports on digital space. Here is the Report for 2022: ► https://wearesocial.com/au/blog/2022/01/digital-2022-another-year-of-bumper-growth/

If you're reading this after that, then I suggest you go to their website and look at the latest.

At the start of 2022, the world's population was 7.89 billion with the United Nations reporting that this figure is growing by 1% per year. Around 5.32 billion people were using a mobile phone (approximately 67% of the world's population). Meanwhile 5 billion people globally used the internet, up by 4.1% from the previous year. Approximately 4.65 billion people were using social media—growing by 326 million over the previous 12 months, with the number of social media users equivalent to more than 58.7% of the world's total population.

I took these figures from The Digital 2022 Global Overview Report [► https://wearesocial.com/digital-2022]—a report comes out every year and it is a fascinating read. It is an excellent source to quickly get a picture of what's happening online.

What Do We Mean by Publishing Online?

When we think of publishing and online, the first thing that often comes to mind is e-books. But publishing online encompasses much more than books. In our digital era, pretty much anything that can be printed on paper is found digitally—whether that's shop catalogues, the instruction manual for your washing machine, the programme for an upcoming conference, a course handbook and so on. These are just a few examples of the plethora of content found and published online. In this book, I'll be referring to many and varied forms of online publishing and digital media. In some instances, the advice will be relevant to all forms and, in some chapters, I will be referring specifically to particular publishing forms.

A Short History of Publishing Online

On 4 July 1971, a digital copy of the US Declaration of Independence was published online (remember Project Gutenberg I mentioned earlier?) enabling people across the global to access it for free. This was a game changer. Since then, publishers have been eager to explore different ways of distributing information simply and easily. The 1980s saw magazine and newspaper publishers experimenting with the use of CDs (in an age when internet usage wasn't as entrenched as it is now) to distribute their editions. The 1990s experienced an accelerated adoption of the internet, with usage growing, and alongside of this, the emergence of the e-book reader. By the late 1990s, the first e-bookstores began to appear.

1

An e-book (short for electronic book) is a book-length publication made available in digital format, consisting of text, images, or both. It is readable on a computer or transferred to a device such as computer, laptop, smart phone, tablet, or dedicated e-book reader (such as the Amazon Kindle and Rakuten Kobo). There is no limit to the topics and genres available online, and includes fiction, non-fiction, autobiographical, how-to, white papers, research studies, and much more. Basically, if it was available in paper print form, it is bound to find its way online.

And if we consider other formats—such as newspapers, magazines, and journals—very few now exist only as physical printed publications. My smartphone gives me access to newspapers from across the global, magazines on every topic imaginable, and even journals and academic publications will generally have an online version.

The Rise of the E-book

The first e-book reader was the Rocket eBook. It was launched in 1998 as the first dedicated e-book reader by NuvoMedia. The investors supporting NuvoMedia were Barnes & Noble and Bertelsmann.

By the 2000s, digital publishing was developing at a rapid pace. In 2003, ePaper technology became available and shortly afterwards, digital reading devices began to appear—such as the Sony Libre and the Amazon Kindle in 2007.

While the original e-books were designed for reading on computers, eReaders revolutionised the book reading market. Suddenly readers could store a greater magnitude of books on a device small enough to fit in their pocket. Google and its search engine also impacted the e-publishing development by scanning thousands of documents and books from various universities, converting the texts into PDF files. They then created Google Books, a unique database and search engine, enabling global readers to read and download (for free) several millions of scanned documents (which do not violate copyright).

The year 2010 saw the introduction of the first iPad by Apple, further changing the way readers could access publications. Rather than files produced specifically for e-readers, readers were now able to use native apps and cross-platform solutions to access their publications; often on the same devices they would access their emails, engage with social media, chat with their friends and family, and so forth. Clearly the market has changed forever and with it the potential opportunities for writers.

The Future for Publishing Online?

A quick browse online into the popularity of e-books and online publishing, and you will find mixed messages. Over the past twenty years or so, since the launch of eReaders, its popularity has varied. As you might expect, in the beginning, some people were eager to try out the new technology. E-books are most popular in China. Apparently in 2020, more than half of Germans bought a printed book. In the US, over the past 10 years the popularity of printed books has waned; however in 2019, 65% of people read a print book compared to only 25% for reading an e-book.

With this in mind, it is probably a reasonable assumption to say e-books are complementary rather than completely replacing the printed publishing industry. How long this will be the case can only be speculated on, and as I said at the start, there is something satisfyingly tactile about sitting down or curling up in bed with a good book. However, a colleague of mine, a longstanding bibliophile, confessed he likes reading Hilary Mantel's epic Tudor books on Kindle because the Kindle is lighter to hold than the books themselves. When asked about it, he confessed he was a convert. For many practical and frankly sensible reasons, e-books are here to stay.

But, of course, we cannot ignore how ingrained smartphones are in our lives. There's no ignoring the benefits of having your favourite magazine edition, or book, on your phone or e-reader, versus carrying around a weighty printed version. But there's been some interesting consequences to our willingness to use this technology—such as needing a break from it. If you have spent all day working before a computer (which, let's face it, many of us must do) and then used your smartphone to keep in touch with your friends, family, and social media, reading a printed book can be a welcome break. Many a student has told me that after a day on their laptops and phones, it's a real joy just to read something on paper. But as is often the case with such things, manufacturers of e-readers have been quick to respond to readers' needs—such as eye strain concerns—introducing features such as e-ink screens.

How Writers and Readers Interact in a Digital World

It's time to address that elephant in the room—you may be thinking it already, so I'm going to declare in this chapter: Isn't there a stigma attached to being an author who is published online? I will even go further and ask—can you still even call yourself a writer? Let alone (gasp) an author?

This one is easy to answer. Provided your writing is high quality and not riddled with mistakes (and I mean here both in the basics such as punctuation and word usage and with the craft of writing), and it is published online, then you are a published writer. So long as you apply the same standards as you would when published down the more traditional printed path, then you can be proud of your online publications. There are some writers who exist solely online—it works for them, and they've built up a reader base who are willing to buy their next e-book. At various writing conferences I have attended, I've met writers who have found success by focusing on publishing online. Some turned to the online marketplace because they had become frustrated and disillusioned with traditional publishers. Others dabbled, got their work published online, and wondered why it wasn't a huge success. It became clear to me that those who made it work, took the time and effort to understand the online marketplace and used it to its full potential to promote their work.

1

I have to say, the self-published writers who I've met tend to fall into two types. The first I will call the online publishing embracers. They love it and dedicate a lot of time and energy into understanding how well (or not) their work is performing. They regularly check the statistics for number of readers, downloads, sales, and so on, and are prepared to try a range of techniques. They will experiment with different digital platforms and try different prices using promotional techniques. These online publishing embracers all say one thing—that it's time-consuming, and you must invest the effort. It is not easy and you need to be prepared to try something and if it doesn't work, try a different approach. They'll often see this as their full-time job.

Are there pitfalls to avoid? Most definitely, and we are going to discuss the key ones in this book. Rush into it and put work out there that isn't a high standard, and it might come back to bite you when you make a name for yourself.

You might still find a publisher who isn't keen on self-published writers, but I'd argue this is becoming rare. So long as you can show your self-publishing has been a worthwhile endeavour, most publishers would see it as a positive that you have already been out there marketing yourself and your work, and you have a valuable reader base. And the reality is, most writers who are published via the traditional path (with a publisher and in print), will end up with the book also available as an e-book.

The second category I will call the online publishing 'sit back and wait' writers. The internet is beyond massive—and if you have ever tried to browse online, such as you might in a bookstore, it is a very different experience. And the writer who thinks they can make a book available online (either uploading it themselves or paying a company to do so), will quickly learn the hard way that, when it comes to having a digital presence, readers won't suddenly find your work. If you are not prepared to dedicate time (or money and pay someone else) to do the supporting tasks that are required to promote your work, then it is going to sit on the metaphorical dusty dark bottom shelf of the online bookstore, never to see the light of day (or the eyes of potential readers).

Reasons to Publish Online

The Subject/Genre of Your Piece Performs Well Online

You have done your research and you can see the subject/genre of your piece is popular with digital audiences. This means that you'll be able to reach out to your audience and it's a format they'll be comfortable using to purchase and read your book. And if it performs well online, you might even sell better via digital platforms than in a traditional bookstore.

That doesn't mean that you can't publish your work online if it is a niche audience and not popular online, but it just means you will need to consider other approaches to help market your e-publication and reach potential audiences.

The Piece Is Better Suited to Digital Platforms

There are some markets that simply do better online. Take for example, articles written on the latest gadgets and technology. Sure, you'll find them in traditional magazines and publications, but there are also loads of websites dedicated to such subjects. And let's face it—where do most of us turn to today when we're after advice? I think it's fair to say that online we are offered quick and immediate advice, which in my experience is pretty good.

These days, you don't have to choose between being an online or traditional writer. Rather than thinking about whether you want to be an 'online' writer, think about your piece and where you think it's best to publish it.

You Want to Be in the Driving Seat of Your Writing Career

There's no denying, even if you're a best-selling established author, if you have an agent and are published by a mainstream publishing company, they will want to have some say in what you write. And it's probably fair to say they have a good reason to, given they probably have insight into the industry. However, this doesn't suit all writers. Some desire the flexibility to write about what they want, without having to cater to the requirements of others. This is where publishing online can give you more freedom.

I met an online author at a conference who had developed such a substantial online following that he made his living writing one e-book a month. That's one heck of a turnover and even today, I wonder how he managed to write and edit a book so quickly. I suspect that he kept the length shorter than your typical novel and he had a formula to his books. Another author I know designs her stories in such a way that every 2 months she releases the next book in her series. Both are great examples of successful writers who make a good living from their writing. What's key is that they really got to know what their online readers wanted—and they give it to them.

Want to Be Your Own Boss

You would like the freedom to publish your work the way you envisage it. Let's face it, if you are at the beginning of your writing career, you are not likely to get a load of freedom when it comes to getting published traditionally. I asked a friend recently how much input she had in the cover of her book (she won a coveted prize, by the way)—she said, 'very little'. She didn't mind and was happy to go with her publisher's recommendations but I have other writer friends who want to maintain this level of control.

1

You Have Tried the Traditional Route to Publishing and Got No Interest

If this is the case, it is important to consider why this might be. Get some feedback from other writers and readers if you are not getting any replies at all. It is a tough path to getting published and it is not uncommon to get frustrated and tired. There are plenty of self-published authors who have successfully proven to traditional publishers they were wrong. Amanda Hocking is the bestselling author of the *Trylle* trilogy and six additional self-published novels. After selling over a million copies of her books, primarily in e-book format, she is widely considered the exemplar of self-publishing success in the digital age. She had almost given up when she decided to give online publishing a shot.

Wanting to Supplement an Established Writing Career

You can be both. Gone are the days where authors were primarily one or the other. Being flexible in regard to publishing online or in paper can provide the opportunity to try out a different market, or experience with a different genre.

Revive a Flagging Publishing Career

It can happen. We've all heard the stories of the struggling writer who had a brilliant idea that got discovered. But we are not all best-selling authors and sadly sometimes those grand visions the publishers had don't eventuate. You can give up or you could try something new. The nice thing about online publishing is that you can call the shots—want to try a different cover? Go for it. The blurb's a little flat—rewrite it. Changes like this can be made quickly when you are publishing online.

More Money

Yep—surely a very strong reason is to take a bigger piece of your metaphorical book pie. The more parties involved, the more that pie must be shared between. If you can take charge and do a lot of (the online publishing) work yourself, it makes a big difference to the proportion you get.

If you have got the necessary IT skills, you are creative, have some ideas for marketing—and you have got the time and money - then why not use your own skills and capabilities rather than pay someone else?

You Want to Get to Market Quickly

Let's face it, publishing via the traditional route isn't a speedy process and perhaps your idea needs to get to market quickly (e.g., maybe it is written about an event that is coming up on an anniversary). Musicians have been doing it for years with streaming and downloads. A new song can be online within 10 min of recording it (maybe sooner if they don't stop for a cup of tea).

Use It as a Springboard to Traditional Publishing

If you can prove that your book has interest and a credible fan base, a publisher will certainly be more interested in you.

When Not to Publish Online

As much as publishing online has opened up many opportunities, there are instances when it might not be the right option. It is important to give it due consideration. Here are some instances where publishing online isn't the way to go:

- If a publisher or agent has given you feedback that your book needs more work, it is wise to take on board what they have to say. They know the market (including online). And if they advise that it's not quality copy, you need to listen. All readers demand quality writing, whether that's on paper or online. If you think you can get away with poor writing online because there are less 'gatekeepers' to stop you publishing, you need to revise your strategy. Poor writing can become a bad smell that just won't go away - it's your reputation at stake!
- You think it is going to be easy. Let's knock this one on the head. It is not easy and it will be time-consuming, and you need to be prepared to try a range of approaches.
- You think it's not going to take up much time. Another one that I'm going to dismiss very quickly. If you want to outsource much of the work to a company then this might be true (but what you save in time you'll pay in money). Publishing online takes time and that's not just in the initial work of getting your manuscript online ready. If you want your book to sell and go on selling, then you need to invest time in marketing and promotional activities.
- Your book is so great it is going to sell itself. Sorry, I hate to be the one to tell you this, but no matter how great your e-book is, readers won't find it (and read it) unless you are prepared to put some serious marketing muscle behind it.

1

❓ **EXERCISE 1: Research About Writing Online**

▶ https://wearesocial.com/au/blog/2022/04/more-than-5-billion-people-now-use-the-internet/

Take a look at this graph from We Are Social (link above). It shows how the global community is using the internet. Read through this list and consider how this might influence what you write for an online audience.

For example, 60% of people use the internet to find information. If I was a blogger, this might tell me something about what people might like to find on my blog. I can also see that researching products and brands is 45%. So if I want to make money from my blog, perhaps I could promote related products or services.

■ **CHECKLIST: Publishing Online**

What is your book, article, poem, paper, post about?	If you haven't written it yet, then this would be a list of what you'd like to write about. To get started you need to know some basics: – What's the topic/subject? – What's the format (poem, article, list, short story etc.)? – Who's your audience? – What's the aim? Informative? Entertainment? Lightv reading? – What's your aim? To make money? Build interest? Test the water? Build your reputation? Gain experience?
Research	This step will take time and it's important to invest in doing it well. Once you get started, it's easy to get either (1) overwhelmed (and give up) or (2) very excited (and want to submit to every site you come across). Please don't do either of these. The next chapter is on the process of researching for publishing online. We'll walk through how to find sites and evaluate whether they are a good match to you and your piece.
Read and understand the submission guidelines	Just because you like the site and there appears to be a good match to your subject matter, doesn't mean they are the right match for you. You need to carefully read through all of their terms and conditions—this includes copyright—and check that you are happy with them. If not, move on. They are not going to change their terms for you.
Prepare your submissions	You've decided on the site you want to submit to, so you accept their terms and conditions, now you need to turn to their website page on submission guidelines. These aren't there as a maybe—you need to conform to these. If they say up to 2000 words, don't think you can submit 2100 and they won't notice. Trust me, they will. Check their guidelines carefully. If they ask for a specific font and size—use it. If they want it submitted as a Word document, that's what you do. If it must be submitted by a deadline—plan to submit it a few days beforehand, just in case. No one wants to work with someone who is difficult, so demonstrate you've read their guidelines and happy to oblige - it definitely gives you an edge over the person who doesn't!

Proofread and edit check	You might think your piece is ready to go but they are serious when they say it must be proofread and edited. This could be the reason your piece gets rejected. Allow yourself time to give the piece a thorough proofread and edit check. Editors are busy people who receive a high volume of submissions. There's nothing more frustrating than coming across a submission that's a great idea but let down by poor craftsmanship. We'll talk about networking in a later chapter, but if you have some writer buddies, checking each other's work is hugely valuable (and I can't recommend a 'buddy system' high enough—I used one for this book).
Submit your piece	Again—follow their guidance. If they ask that it be send to a particular email address or on a web page—that's what you need to do.
Follow-up	What if you don't hear anything? My advice is to give it a reasonable timeframe—if you've had no acknowledge of receipt, after a week you could send a polite email just to check it arrived. If they say no, then it's very unlikely that anything you say will change their mind. It's disappointing, but there are many online platforms and publishers to consider, so put that energy into finding another one.
Your piece is accepted	Great! You've got there but you're probably not quite finished with the piece. It's possible they'll want some changes—my advice is to be open to their suggestions but if something is very important to you, then don't compromise. It comes down to how important it is versus getting your piece published.

Publishing Online: Getting Started

Contents

© The Author(s), under exclusive license to Springer Nature
Switzerland AG 2023
L. Kesteven, *Publishing Online for Writers*,
https://doi.org/10.1007/978-3-031-21366-3_2

About this Chapter

In this chapter we will:
- Cover the stages of publishing online and building a digital presence
- Discuss how a writer can assess if their work is publication ready
- Consider how to take that first leap when publishing online
- Explore pitfalls to avoid
- EXERCISE: Pitch Perfect
- CHECKLIST: Preparing to Publish Online

Where to Start

Writers will typically approach publishing online in two ways. They may have written a piece and then decide they want to publish it online, or they first find somewhere that is accepting online submission and write the piece according to their specifications and requirements. You'll find variations—for example, you might write a piece that you think is interesting, and before continuing you decide to check out the market to see if there is potential for publishing it. Regardless of whether you think you have a completed piece or not, it's very unlikely that you can publish it just as it. Most sites will have requirements—perhaps it's word length, or language, or style—and your piece will probably need some adapting to make it publishable.

Whether you have a piece in mind or you're simply interested in getting published online, the starting point is the same.

Know Your Market

Regardless of your subject or topic, or where you want to publish it's essential to know your market and potential readers. We know readership online is growing, but by how much?

Let's go back to the WeAreSocial report again:
- ► https://wearesocial.com/au/blog/2022/01/digital-2022-another-year-of-bumper-growth/

In April 2022:
- The world's population was 7.89 billion with the United Nations reporting that this figure is growing by 1% per year.
- 5.32 billion people were using a mobile phone (approximately 67% of the world's population).
- Meanwhile 5 billion people globally used the internet, up by 4.1% from the previous year.
- 4.65 billion people were using social media—growing by 326 million over the previous 12 months, with the number of social media users equivalent to more than 58.7% of the world's total population.

And we can see that over half of the global popular are active social media users. That's a 10.1% increase from the previous year. So I guess it's reasonable to say that there are definitely readers online. There's a lot of useful information in their report, such as the most popular social platforms so I'd recommend that you take a look (and do so each year so that you can see trends).

Preparing to Publish Online

If you skip preparation, there's a very high probability that your submission will be rejected. No matter how amazing your piece is, the reality is that digital platforms who receive online submissions, are receiving a large volume on a daily basis (just as you found their website, so too will have other writers from across the globe). They may have very small editorial teams (if they have them at all) and simply don't have time to edit and format a piece to fit their requirements. So, if you ignore their submission guidelines, don't be surprised if they're not interested. On the other hand, if you do conform to their guidelines, you are beginning the relationship by making a good impression.

Deciding where to submit your piece is a critical part of the process. The better the match, the better your chance of being successful, so it's worth taking your time to find sites/digital platforms that are seeking submissions like yours. You might find a site you like and would really like to be published on, but if you don't meet their requirements, then you're better putting your effort into a site that is a better match (or revising your piece to meet their guidelines). Taking the time now will save a lot of effort (and heartache) in the future.

Six Steps to Publish Online

1. Identify the topic or niche of your piece
2. Identify format
3. Write a pitch
4. Identify likely online audience/s
5. Determine your aim from publishing online
6. Research potential digital platforms/websites

1. What's the Topic or Niche of Your Piece?

If you don't have a piece and you're researching to find ideas, jot down a list of areas that you could write about. You don't always need to be an expert to write a credible piece. Here are just a few examples:
- If you recently purchased a house/car/bike/scooter then you know, first hand, some of the hurdles faced. This can be useful advice for someone about to

embark on the same process. If you're upfront and say you're not an expert but have recently had the experience, then your readership understand you're sharing your knowledge, not as an expert, but as someone who has 'done it before'.

- Finance. Maybe you're a student with a tight budget—you could offer advice to new students who are suddenly faced with having to live off very limited funds. Maybe you've recently started up a small business and can share your experiences of the financial costs of setting up a new enterprise. Be clear that you're not a financial expert and cannot offer expert advice simply that you are sharing your own experiences.
- Travel. You don't have to travel far to write a travel piece. It could be about your local area and aimed at visitors. Don't have funds? Aim it at the budget traveller.
- Fitness. Just started running? Jumping? Skipping? Weightlifting? Boxing? Share the things you're learning along the way. Others will be interested in your journey, regardless of whether you're just starting out or an expert. What's important is that you're clear from the onset. For example, I'm not an experienced runner and I'm going to share my knowledge, the good and the bad. Again, be clear about your experience and if you want to be really helpful, provide links to other useful sites.
- Medical. Struggling with a knee injury? Again, share your journey with others, especially what has and hasn't worked for you. Again, just be clear it's your shared experiences and that you're not an expert.
- Personal development. Maybe you've experienced the highs and lows of online dating. Or you've recently gone through a breakup. You might think it's been done before but it's possible you've got an interesting take on it.
- Relationships. You don't need to be a counsellor to share your experiences with others. Just be upfront about exactly what your piece/blog is about and that you're not a relationship counsellor (unless of course, you are).
- Lifestyle. I've recently gone from living in a rural village to an inner-city suburb. It's taken a lot of adjusting and it would have been helpful to hear from others how to make that transition. Lifestyle is a huge category that's constantly changing with trends coming and going. If you want to contribute your writing then you need to stay current with what's happening - or even better, predict what might happen next.
- The latest gadget. If you've recently upgraded your phone or maybe acquired a fitness device—share you experience. But be quick, others are also keen to write about what's new and shiny.
- Food. Yep, there's loads of sites out there but there's also lots of readers. Maybe you've recently become vegan and can offer advice to others in your area on what to eat and where to buy certain foods. And you don't need to be a fancy chef to write about cooking—maybe you could offer advice to those who need to whip up healthy meals, quickly and on a budget.
- Entertainment. You name it—the latest games, films, series, books—share your take on it. Maybe you have a niche—could you focus on particular games, films in a particular genre, the latest blockbuster series not to be missed. Rather than writing about horror films, could you be more specific? Focus in on a particular era or type of horror film.

- Pets. This isn't about the obvious; if you're a pet owner you'll understand that you can suddenly need advice on all different types of things. When I recently acquired a second cat, I found myself in the midst of a territorial battlefield. Not something I go through often, but I very much appreciated the advice I found from an informative cat blogger.
- Fashion. This doesn't have to be on the latest trends. Maybe you could offer advice to a student on a budget, or someone who is about to start their first job.

2. What Is the Format of Your Piece?

Is it:
- An article? If so, what is the subject? What's the tone?
- A short story?
- Piece of prose?
- Poem?
- Non-fiction?
- An academic paper?
- A novel?
- Training material?
- Self-help guide?
- Podcast?

3. What's Your Pitch?

Before you can start looking for potential sites and digital platforms to submit your work to, you'll need to identify what your piece is about. Just as you would for a submission to a traditional publishing or literary agency, you need to be able to briefly and succinctly articulate what your work is about. You might have heard the term 'elevator pitch'. It can be applied in many contexts, from a business project through to a film. The basic idea is that you are in the elevator with someone who asks what your work is about and you have the time it takes to get to their floor to explain it to them. So it needs to be short, succinct, and memorable. You want them getting out of the elevator thinking—wow, what a great idea.

Sometimes it's clear—it's a magazine article on travelling around Spain with young children, or it's a poem about springtime on the east coast of America, or it's a mental health paper on coping with anxiety in your first year at university— these examples have a clear topic and we can see what the form is. But sometimes it's not quite so straightforward—maybe it's a poem written by someone who has struggled with anxiety. Or it's a short story that is set in Barcelona. Maybe it's a fictional story based on a person's life. Or maybe the piece crosses multiple genres. These are just a few examples that demonstrate it's not always clear-cut. If you're not sure then write down all the possibilities—these will all be useful as you'll see

2

shortly when we start to investigate what opportunities are available. As you start your research you can decide how you want to shape the piece.

If you're pitching to a particular publication then your starting point is to check their guidelines. They will likely tell you exactly what they want. If you can't find it on their website (if they don't have a dedicated page try FAQ or Contact Us), check if they have a blog, and if you still can't locate it, try a search with the site's name and 'submission guidelines'. If you still can't find it, move on.

4. Who Is Your Likely Audience?

It's possible your piece will appeal to a wide audience, but it can help to narrow down your site search if you understand who you are targeting. In the example I have used above on the mental health piece on coping with anxiety, it's likely that it will have been written for a particular audience - for example, coping with anxiety as a child, or a teenager, a young adult, and so on When you come to submitting your piece, one of the questions that is likely to be put to you is: who is your audience.

'You have to consider the audience. Basically the first thing I consider now is what the audience's experience is going to be, and when is the audience's bladder at bursting point. When are they bored?' (Taika Waititi).

5. Why Do You Want to Publish This Piece?

It's very possible you're responding: I want to get paid! Who wouldn't! And if writers are ever going to make a living (and by this I mean earn enough to pay the rent/mortgage, eat, buy clothes, maybe even go on a holiday from time to time), then it's reasonable to ask to be paid for your services. And let's face it, being a good writer is a talent and providing high quality copy/content is a valued service. So, you should definitely get paid, and a reasonable and fair sum. But when it comes to payment, sometimes this will come in different forms. Ideally it's monetary (and if you're a full-time writer living off your earnings then it will mostly need to be) but sometimes there are valid reasons to have a piece published and not receive a monetary payment because there are other benefits that are worth something to you.

What's a fair monetary payment? That will very much depend on what is it you're writing and who will be publishing it. It's a marketplace, driven by supply and demand. If there's enough demand, sites will want to publish your work and (hopefully) pay for it. How much can you expect to be paid? It doesn't really work that way unless you are a well-recognised writer. Most writers will look around and compare what sites are offering. And even then, it's not always a straightforward decision to go with the site that pays the most. It may be more beneficial long term to be published on a well-respected site and earn less, because it improves your reputation.

Other Benefits to Publishing Online that are not Monetary

Should you consider publishing your work on sites that don't pay? There are some situations where it can be worthwhile.

Gaining Experience

Especially when a writer is starting out, it can seem a huge leap to having your work published. As a university lecturer of creative writing students, I was very keen that first year students be taught how to publish online. Why? Because it very quickly gets them into the writing world—they get to experience a publishing process, they can interact with other writers and with readers, they get feedback, but very importantly, seeing your writing in a published form is motivating.

Building a Reputation

Does publishing online count and make you a writer? You bet it does! And the more you can list as being published, the more of a portfolio you're building up. And the more readers you have, the more people that know about your writing—so you'd better make sure it's high quality! It's about building up a portfolio of quality work and a digital presence. Promoting yourself as a writer when all you have is a few blog posts is probably going to raise eyebrows, but if you've had an active blog with regular contributions over 12 months, plus articles published on online magazine sites, then people can quickly see that you take your writing seriously.

Build a Network

If you think you're competing with other writers online, think again. Other writers, especially those with blogs and are busy getting articles published, will often link to other content. Working together is, a way to increase the reach of your piece. That's not to say that there aren't people out there who will copy work and portray it as their own, but a little research and caution will hopefully help you spot the people to avoid. Again, do your research and check the person out online before making any commitments. If they are working in a credible network and regularly connecting with other writers, that's a good sign.

A Writer Needs Readers

Okay, that's not exactly true—there are writers who perhaps write solely for their own purposes—but I think it's fair to say that most writers want their work to be read. There's no better place than to find readers than online. But bear in mind—while there are many readers to be found via the web—not all of them will be true, honest, or kind (and trolls can be very unkind just for the sake of being unkind).

Meet Other Writers

Writers are readers to, and if you can engage with a writers' community, it can be hugely beneficial. Not only for feedback, but for the social aspect. There's no better shoulder to cry on when you receive a rejection email than that of another writer who has been through the same experience. By working together, you can provide each other with advice (avoid that site, it wasn't a great experience, or this site is accepting submissions) as well as feedback on writing.

2

Test Out an Idea

This can be very helpful if you're experimenting with a new idea and not sure if there's appeal in it.

There are some writing platforms where stories are serialised and released on a weekly/monthly/other basis. If your readership builds and you have readers eager for the next instalment, you know your idea is working. It's also a great way to engage with own readership and make them feel involved.

A quick online search will reveal numerous experiences of writers who were rejected by traditional publishers but then went on to prove them wrong by their popularity online. A huge benefit of the digital world is that it can reach a lot of readers - just remember they'll all have different viewpoints and reasons for providing feedback (some helpful and others just plain nasty).

Gain Feedback

It may seem risky to engage with strangers when it comes to your writing but sometimes they'll be more honest than your friends or family. Just remember, they don't know you so don't take it personally. And be realistic and only take on board what you think is valuable.

Enhance Your Writing Craft

Now I'm not advocating that you publish poor quality work—in fact I'm saying the opposite—don't publish your work online until it's great quality. But the more you write and share, the more feedback you'll receive, and your writing craft will improve.

6. Research Potential Digital Platforms and Media

In the subsequent chapters in Part I, I will explore these in more detail, but for now here's a list of potential digital platforms to consider online. But let's begin by understanding what a digital platform is. In it's simplest form, it is an online space where users can interact, collaborate, and transact with each other and/or digital content. This might be to find or share information or to buy products/services. Digital platforms include websites, mobile applications, social media networks, and online marketplaces.

Online Magazines

There are hundreds if not thousands of online magazines on just about every topic you can image. Some are high quality with a well-recognised reputation and strong readership. On the other end of the scale, are some that are downright dodgy. So, you need to do your research. Are we going to list sites in this publication? No. For two good reasons. The first is that the digital marketplace changes rapidly, so if we included a list today, it will likely have changed tomorrow. And the second reason is that I don't know what your piece or article is about, so I can't advise what sites would be suitable for you—you'll need to do your research! What's important is to do your research about a site that you are interested in before submitting your work. People love to share their experiences online—especially if they've been bad. So find out if others have had good or bad experiences.

If you're looking for free sites, there are many available online (try typing 'Free Article Submission Sites').

In ▶ Chap. 3 we'll explore this in more detail.

Online Journals

Journals are typically for academic papers but you don't necessarily need to be an academic to have a published paper. You may be a student or an expert in the field with practical experience. The main difference between an article in a magazine and a paper in a journal is the style. A journal paper is more formal in style, likely to be longer (not always), and addresses a particular question or topic.

I started investigating journals when I was midway through my doctorate. Partly because it was helpful to understand the style of an academic paper but also because I was interested to see which online journals might be interested in my own work later on. I'll use my work as a good example of how it's not always straightforward. I am a writer of historical fiction so there were a few obvious matches: journals on creative and critical writing, journals on the craft of novel writing, journals on writing on history. But the more I researched, the more I realised that my work crossed into other areas. For example, part of my studies was in the area of Pierre Bourdieu (and the application on his sociological theories to writing) and there are journals firmly based in the field of Sociology which are interested in how such theories have been applied in other areas. My novel is historical and set in the world of art in the sixteenth century—another aspect that I explore when investigating journals and resulting in me presenting a paper at a conference for art historians. You might think I'm contradicting myself here—didn't I say earlier in this chapter that it's important to find a good match? That's right, it's very important, but be open to what that good match might be. A good match, when it comes to academic journals, is likely to be something that triggers their interest, something new and innovative. For example, the application of Bourdieu's theories in the development of a novel hasn't been hugely explored—so when I met a Bourdieu scholar, he was very interested in my work. Sometimes the obvious route—which for me would have been creative and critical writing—probably has a lot of similar papers on writing historical fiction.

Top tip: Try to find what is unique and interesting about your piece or is a new perspective on a subject well discussed.

In ▶ Chap. 4 we'll explore this in more detail.

Businesses

Businesses with a digital presence often have a need for content and this means they are on the lookout for writers who produce quality work/copy. What do I mean by quality copy? It's means that your copy (whether that's an article, text for a website, recorded words for a podcast) is well crafted, easy to understand, mistake free, interesting to read, and has not been published elsewhere. Let's say you've written several articles on looking after a new puppy. You could try an online magazine on dogs but it's very likely they have published on this subject before and received many articles on that very subject. So why not try looking a bit wider. For example, a veterinary surgery with a website may be looking to include regular articles on pet care, or you might find a local dog groomer who has a blog. It's about finding a connection. Travel writing is a very popular area—let's face it, who wouldn't fancy visiting foreign locations and getting paid to write about it. If you're very very lucky, The Lonely Planet might offer you a job, but (back on planet earth) most of us won't be that lucky. Rather than giving up, explore other options—airline magazines (yep, those ones we all find in the pocket on the seat in front of us) are published every month and in need of interesting articles. It's not the most exciting media but it's a great start to getting published. Maybe it's a blog for new students who have just moved to a city to study—an article on places to visit in the area that are free or don't cost a fortune might be just the thing.

Top tip: Think beyond the obvious (which has often been done before way too many times).

Retailers

Yep, retailers are businesses with either websites or sold via other digital platforms. I've given them their own section because retailers are often trying to attract buyers with more than just product catalogues. They want to give their followers something more. Crumpler are a great example of this—they are a retailer that sells bags—but if you take a look at their website you'll see it contains more than just bags—it's promoting a lifestyle. They have a blog on their website with articles on places to visit, wildlife, conservation. They know their market and who they want to appeal to. Retailers are embracing the digital world and are keen to create a digital space for their buyers—one that provides them with valuable information and a place where they'll return to because they trust the brand.

Local Publications

There are many digital platforms that are focused on an area—for example, it might be a town or city, or it could be for a community, such as a university or a group that shares a particular interest. One publication that I have written for is the National Childbirth Trust magazine for my area. Many towns will have numerous publications (often online) and they are looking for relevant and regular content. You might come across a website for a group of runners in your city and it's possible they want content that will interest their group and encourage new members. That might be on running, but it could also be on places to go running, dealing with injuries, and so on. Having regular, high quality content is a constant demand for any organisation with a digital presence. The aim is to drive traffic to their website and to build a connection with their readership, who will then hopefully buy their products or services.

Blogs

Can you get paid for writing blog posts? Yes, there are sites out there that will pay for posts. Generally speaking, the sites that pay are after high quality content that is unique and innovative. They're not interested in content that can easily be found on other sites. So think about any skills or niche areas that you can write about. Some good examples include:

- Technology blogs. They are often seeking content on the latest developments and products. Maybe you're good at programming languages and can offer advice or write tutorials to others. The most in demand will be for products or releases that have just come out.
- Finance blogs. If you can do some research and write about latest trends and offer credible advice on savings, investments, and other finance subjects, then they just might be interested. Understand the marketplace - for example, if interest rates are on the increase, readers might be interested in an article on property investments areas that are expected to grow.
- Travel blogs. There are loads out there—and not just sites dedicated to places. There are sites that focus on particular interests (such as hiking holidays), or travel styles (such as solo travellers, families, adventure travellers, budget, festival), or demographics (such as the 18–35 or senior travellers). There will be plenty of competition, so make sure your piece is interesting, unique, and well-written. Pieces don't need to be specifically on travelling—think broader on topics such as history, local wildlife, geography, and nature history.
- Blogs on writing. You might think this topic has been exhausted but if you're creative, you can often come up with a new angle that will capture interest.
- Niche blogs. You name it, there is probably a blog for it. I once had a student who was struggling to find a blog that matched her skills. The first week she came in with a site for dogs—only problem was she had never owned a dog and didn't know much about them. The next week, it was a site about her local town. I ask her to list five posts she could write and she ran out of ideas at three. The following week she surprised us all when she came in with a site dedicated to Death Masks. It turns out she knew a great deal about them. To cut a long story short, this student went on to write a load of posts for them and a great collaboration was born.

❓ EXERCISE 2: Pitch Perfect

Let's write a pitch (this could be for an idea you're working on or for something completely fictitious!)

Why should people read your article?	Why are you passionate about it? And why should other people be passionate about it as well? Is it newsworthy? Why is it important that others should know about this?

2

Why would this publisher/digital platform be interested?	How does it fit in with their purpose? Why would this appeal to their readership?
What's the hook?	In one sentence, convince the editor/digital platform representative they must publish this.
Main points	Just two or three but no more, and again, it must be succinct.
What's your point of view?	This might be your angle or context.
Why you?	Why are you the person to write this? Keep it brief and relevant. One sentence is perfect.

■ **CHECKLIST: Preparing to Publish Online**

What is your topic or niche?	If you have written the piece, it's important to really understand what it's about. It's not enough to say—it's a piece on Where to Eat in Bali. Think about the focus of the piece—for example, is it for travellers or locals? Those on a budget or those wanting to splurge? A particular dietary requirement—such as gluten free? If you haven't written the piece yet think about it in broad terms—where is your expertise? In my example above, if you know Bali well, where is your specialism when it comes to eating out? Was it at local food markets or in fine restaurants? So, think about what could you write about?
Identify format	There are different ways of publishing your piece. An article, with some modifications can become a blog post or podcast. And don't forget that Digital Platforms will have requirements—such as word length and style. If you haven't written your piece think about what you'd like to do and the possible formats you'd like to explore.
Write a pitch	Always check the guidelines of the site you're submitting to. If they say they like the format of 'Top 10' then include this in your pitch. Keep it succinct, engaging, and to the point. What is your piece about?
Identify likely audiences	Come up with a list of who would be interested in reading your piece. Consider why they'd be interested and what is new/unique about your article that they wouldn't find somewhere else
What's your aim from publishing this piece?	Monetary gain is an obvious one but there can be other reasons. Getting your foot in the door should not be ignored. If you've already been published by a digital platform, they will be more likely to consider you again (especially if your piece proved popular with their readership).
Research potential sites	This one is up to you—I don't know your topic or subject area, but the best place to start is typing that into a search engine and refine, refine, refine. Don't just stick to the formats you are familar with - it's possible that an area has been well explored via one media (such as digital magazines) but less so in another (such as a podcast)

Publishing in Online Magazines

Contents

© The Author(s), under exclusive license to Springer Nature
Switzerland AG 2023
L. Kesteven, *Publishing Online for Writers*,
https://doi.org/10.1007/978-3-031-21366-3_3

About this Chapter

In this chapter we will:

- Consider whether it's worth submitting your work to online magazines that don't pay
- Discuss how to assess if a magazine is for you
- Cover how to publish with a magazine online and the different options
- Outline the steps to go through once you've found a suitable magazine
- EXERCISE: Is it the right magazine?
- CHECKLIST: Magazine Submission

Getting your work published online with magazines is an ever-growing and in-demand market. As more readers move online, the demand for content rises. You'll find online magazines on pretty much any topic you can think of—and then more—and they won't necessarily be called 'magazines'. I'll use the term quite loosely in this chapter and it refers to any online site that accepts articles.

What Makes a Website an Online Magazine?

Online magazines are very similar to print magazines, except that they are available online rather than at a physical newsagent or bookstore (although I edit one which is available in both formats). With improvements in technology, many have online versions that flip pages, such as you would a magazine printed on paper. Today, you'll generally find an online version for most popular magazines. Not surprisingly, the first magazines to appear online were in the areas of computing and technology, probably because it's a digital media they were comfortable with. Online magazines can go by various names, such as ezine or webzine or e-magazine. Many publications that were previously only available in print have gone digital via an online service and charge a fee.

Top tip: Take a look at the online magazines available via Issuu (▶ www.Issuu.com). Issuu is like an online version of a magazine stand.

How Does that Differ from a Journal?

Where an online magazine represents topics of interest to specialists in or societies for academic subjects, science, trade, or industry, these are generally referred to as online journals. The key difference is that these are often papers written by experts who are sharing their knowledge with their communities. I'll cover publishing with an online journal later in the next chapter.

3

What Can You Get Published with an Online Magazine?

It would probably be easier to ask: what can't you get published with an online magazine! With the cost significantly less to setting up an online magazine versus a traditional printed magazine, there are online magazines for virtually any topic or subject you can think of. While it's a global marketplace with publications attracting readers from all over the world, there will be instances where magazines are targeted at a particular readership (for example, a student magazine for a particular university)—but so long as your piece is suited to that readership, then you certainly don't need to be 'local' to submit your work.

That's great news for writers—the more publications there are, the more articles they are publishing, and the more work for writers like you and me. But what it also means is that we need to do our homework because we now compete on a global writers marketplace. We need to research and understand what their magazine is really about, what they are interested in, and who their target audience is. Otherwise, we'll just waste a lot of time submitting to sites that probably won't be interested. Remember they want articles that are unique and innovative; it's very unlikely they'll want an article that is simple rehashing something another site published last month.

Is it Worthwhile Submitting Your Work to Sites that Don't Pay?

This is a question many writers ask themselves, and if you want to actually make a living from your writing, then giving away your services for free can seem like a very bad idea (particularly when you have bills to pay). If you want to make a living (pay the rent/mortage, feed yourself/the family etc) then focusing on those digital platforms that pay is a very sensible approach.

But there can be good reasons to consider a site that doesn't pay:

- It can be a way to test the water and get feedback on your work. For example, you may be experimenting with an idea and not sure whether there is much of a market for it. Putting a piece online is a way of getting feedback—both good and bad. You'll need to develop thick skin as online feedback can be brutal. Sometimes it's nonsense and not worth paying attention to, but you can also get an idea of whether people, in general, are interested.
- Articles can be used to promote your brand—you the writer. It can also be used to promote a business, informational subjects, or your area of expertise. Maybe it's a short story that has some connection to a novel you're about to publish—building up an interested audience who will go on to buy your novel certainly makes it a viable proposition. Publishing online for free as part of your marketing strategy (we will get to this in a later chapter), with a particular goal in mind, can be sensible. Publishing online for no payment without a strategy is simply giving your work away!
- Articles can contain links, and these can be valuable to content writers and bloggers. It's important to understand how linking works. There are two types of links: dofollow and nofollow. A dofollow link passes the authority

of the origin site to the destination site and this is useful when it comes to SEO (search engine optimisation)—or helping your article appear towards the top of a list when people are using search engines. A nofollow doesn't pass on the authority so you won't get the full SEO benefits but they can still generate traffic to a website. In most instances, it's good to find free article submission sites that have a high Alexa domain ranking and allow dofollow links.

- Build up your readership. If you want to get your work published, regardless of the form, then readers are very important. If you can show a publisher that you have a strong following online, with readers eagerly awaiting the next instalment of your online work, then there's a good chance they'll take you seriously. And let's face it, if those future readers end up buying your work, then you're making money from your writing. But it's comes back to having a strategy and a good reason behind publishing your work for free.

Should You Publish Your Article on More than One Site?

You can, but it's generally not a good idea. If the same article appears on different sites, its value decreases. And importantly, search engines won't know which is the authoritative article, so it likely won't be indexed in searches.

Instead of publishing on multiple sites, it's better to use links between related articles. This will increase your readership—and if your links are dofollow, it will improve your ranking in search engines.

When you publish the same article on different sites, it will diminish its value.

Assessing if a Magazine Is for You

Just like you would investigate an area before moving into the neighbourhood, it's important to check out if a magazine site is suited to you. Here are some questions to consider:

Match Made in Heaven?

Editors are looking for articles that will easily fit into their mould. Let's use a travel article to explore this idea and look at some popular online travel magazines.

Wanderlust has the strap line—Taking the Road less travelled. So immediately I know, if I have an article about a visit to the Eiffel Tower, they're probably not going to be interested. On the day I visited their site, this was one of their headliner articles: 'World Heritage: Exploring the Ancient Ksour of Mauritania'. There's also a quiz: 'How much do you know about UK traditions', and five alternative things to do in Northern France (we'll come to list articles later on in this chapter but already an example of their popularity).

The *Culturist* is another travel website. Their strap line is: Travel. Do Good. Live Well. Short but very revealing about the audience they appeal to. Their articles include: 'Together We Can Restore Healthy Oceans', 'Sweat Gold—the Industry of Bananas in Queensland, Australia', and 'Sounds of Seville'.

Butterfly Diaries is a different take again on travel; on the opening page of their website they ask: Tell us your Travel Story, and have travel tips for Newbies. Their sections include Tips and Tricks for Traveling Cheap and Take on the World, one city at a time.

These are a selection from a long list of online magazines about travel and they each have their own look and feel. If my travel article is aimed at the young, first-time traveller, the editor for *Butterfly Diaries* might be more interested than say the *Culturist*. Whereas if my piece has a very conservation angle—maybe it's a piece about saving turtles—then I'd probably try *Culturist*. *Wanderlust* say they're after articles on those more obscure places—and I can see this from their articles. But they also publish pieces about popular places so long as its focus is on alternative things to do.

With each of these examples, from a quick look at their websites we can see the type of traveller they are aimed at. So, you need to take your article and consider if your ideal reader is a good match for the site.

Is Your Piece Original?

No matter how well-crafted your piece is, if the site has published something similar, then they are unlikely to be interested. So, you need to do your research—even if the magazine is exactly the site for you—if they published a similar article recently, they're not going to want to look like they can't come up with new and fresh content. And if the topic of your article has been well published elsewhere, it's unlikely sites will be interested unless you've got a new and interesting angle.

Of course, if you really want to be published by a particular site, you can view this as an opportunity and come up with a revised article. If you can provide a new angle to add to the original piece then you might just catch their eye.

Ease of Use of the Magazine

While it's great to get published, it's even better when you're published on a site that you're really proud to see your work associated with. There are some sites out there that have been poorly designed, where navigation is difficult and articles are hard to find. While your work may be on their site, if people can't find it then it's be a futile exercise.

The best way to assess a magazine is to become a reader and navigate around the website as a reader might. If you don't immediately feel it's a site you'd be proud to send onto your friends and family, then move on.

Alexa Ranking

Checking a site's Alexa ranking can be very useful. The lower the number, the more popular it is. If a site ranks in the top 100,000 sites in the world, it means that it has a high Alexa page rank.

Is Their Genre and Style Suitable for Your Piece?

This is from *Raconteur Magazine*, which describes themselves as a Literary magazine for writers by writers. Here is what they ask for in regard to genre and style:

You could say we're genre and style agnostic. We consider all writing, unless it will appeal only to a handful of people. If your piece is engaging and memorable, you've got a shot. We're not averse to most subject matter—and we have a dark sense of humour—but anything intentionally offensive or distasteful is unlikely to be accepted. We don't publish work intended for children.

▶ https://www.raconteurmag.com/submissions

Black Fox Literary Magazine is a print and online biannual publication, which is interested in fiction and non-fiction. That sounds pretty broad but let's take a closer look:

We accept work based on merit and not based on genre. We enjoy receiving submissions from under-represented genres such as: YA, romance, flash fiction, mystery, etc.

▶ https://www.blackfoxlitmag.com/submit/

These are two good examples of magazines that are clearly outlining what they are looking for in submissions.

Publishing with a Magazine Online

In ▶ Chap. 2, as part of our preparation, we decided what the topic of our writing piece is. To step through the options when researching where to submit our articles to, I'm going to use the example of an article about introducing a second dog into a home with an existing dog. What the article is about isn't important—I'm just using it to demonstrate my points and decisions.

Option 1: A Focused Magazine

In my example, this would be a magazine focused on dogs and aimed at dog owners. I might start off with searching for something along the lines of Dog's World or Dog's Life. You get my drift. Another option would be to walk into a newsagent and see what relevant magazines are on their shelves. But there's a little more to it than simply typing 'dog magazine' into a search engine. Magazines will probably be based somewhere—that doesn't necessarily preclude you from submitting, but it might affect the language you use (such as English vs. American English) and if the magazine is targeted at readers in a particular location (e.g., I just found a dog magazine focused on pet owners in California) then consider if your piece is still relevant. There will be aspects that are specific to a location—for example, in Australia, you cannot take dogs into national parks, whereas in the UK, dogs are welcome (on leashes) in their national parks. This is a good example of knowing your location and ensuring your content is appropriate. In this example, an article on responsible dog walking in national parks would be quite acceptable in a UK-based publication, but certainly not in an Australian-based one!

A good place to start is the magazines that you like to read. Chances are you already know what type of articles these magazines publish and what subjects the magazines have not covered recently. If you don't know/haven't been paying attention, now's the time to get well acquainted.

There are also magazines catering to particular niche areas. For example, publications focused on puppies, working dogs, farm dogs, or show dogs - I could go.

What Are Editors Interested In?

They will usually offer some guidance on their website, so that's the best place to start. But here are some generic tips:

- There needs to be something of interest for others—'what's in it for the reader?' is a good question to ask yourself. I could probably write 2000 words on why I love walking my dog and how fascinating she is but I expect the editors of pet magazines are deluged with such personal stories. That's why my proposed article for this chapter is about something more focused—introducing a second pet into a home isn't something we typically do often, and it can be tricky, so I'm hoping it is something that other pet owners might be interested in.
- What articles have they published already? This will give you an idea of their style—but also, if they've published something similar recently you might need to reconsider your idea or look elsewhere. It's possible you could, with a few tweaks, have it as a follow-up piece.
- What is the publications style? For example, one thing I have noticed is that magazines about pets are mostly upbeat and focused on being helpful. They don't tend to publish stories about beloved pets that have passed away.
- What they are interested in are pieces that will catch their readers' eye, help them, and capture their interest. In the case of pets, this could be about pet care but it needs to be relevant—most pet owners know how to look after their pets but they would potentially be interested in recent advances in health care. They might also find pieces on behaviour issues helpful. I might have just started jogging and want to bring my dog along—so a review of dog leads especially designed for runners, just might capture my attention.
- Events and famous personalities are also topics interesting to editors. How about a local event for pooches? Or an article about the number of celebrities who own dachshunds/collies/labradors? Readers probably don't want to hear about your dog, but they definitely want to know if Johnny Depp has a dog and how his famous pooch lives (we all remember his visit to Australia with his 2 dogs!).

Option 2: General Interest Magazines

Although pet magazines are an obvious choice to submit my article to, many other magazines have room and interest in pet articles. Health magazines may be interested in an article on staying fit with your dog. Family magazines may be interested in how to introduce children to their first puppy. Since the magazine's readership are likely to have pets, any new and scary dog disease might make a great article for a general audience. Just think about stories that would pique the magazine's readers interest.

Let's take a look at *Reader's Digest*—it's been around for a long time (according to their website, since 1922) and has around 80 million readers worldwide. This is from their website:

- MEET everyday heroes, ordinary people who acted bravely in extraordinary situations.
- LEARN about the latest medical advances and scientific discoveries and how they impact your everyday life.
- LAUGH along with the *Reader's Digest* community on our hugely popular humour pages.
- SAVE time, money, or both! With handy tips, tricks, and articles on home, travel, family, food, finance, and more.
- DISCOVER an art you thought you'd lost: The pleasure of reading, absorbing, and sharing ideas.

There is no mention of any particular genre or field. They are looking for articles and creative writing that fits into the criteria above. So, it's possible they'll be interested in my pet article.

I've just taken a look at the *Reader's Digest* submission page in Australia and they were looking (and paying) for:

- A touching, inspiring personal story or life-changing experience (must be true)
- A true account of an act of kindness from strangers
- Anecdotes and Jokes
- Your Deepest Wish
- Smart Animals

(▶ https://www.readersdigest.com.au/customer-care/magazine-submission-faq)
And according to their UK website submissions page, they are interested in:
- An anecdote
- A joke for 'laugh!'
- A story for 'You Couldn't Make it Up'
- My Great Escape

With magazines such as this, it's worth doing a bit more online researching—it's easy enough to do—as we can see that the Australian and UK versions are slightly different. There's nothing stopping you from submitting to a magazine that is located elsewhere—so long as their readership will be interested. There's not much point submitting an article about great places to walk your dog in the South of England, to a magazine based in California and aimed at local readers.

I was looking at the News on my iPhone this morning, and I came across a section dedicated to dogs (as most people find with new technology, it's very smart at knowing my interests). But a number of things caught my eye—first was the types of articles—and second was the magazines they were published in. Let's take a look:

- A hot new private members club for dogs (*The Times*)
- How a dog trainer became a viral star (*People*)
- Trained dogs may be better at detecting Covid than PCR nasal tests (*USA Today*)
- Ten not-so-easy steps to get your dog to take a pill (*The Free Press*)
- I visited a tiny 'Dog Bakery' serving doughnuts and cookies (*Echo*)
- From fighting hamsters to vomiting cats—your pet queries answered (*The Sun*)
- Pete the Vet: My dog is licking his paws—is he stressed? (*Irish Examiner*)

These are all very dog related—and I appreciate that some reading this chapter may not be interested in writing about canines—but stay with me, as the points this example shows applies to any subject, not just pets. In terms of the topics published, they typically fall into one or more of the following categories:

- Very specific. For example—it's not just an article about dogs and stress, but about licking paws
- Unique. Can't say I've heard of a private members club for dogs
- News breaking. Covid detecting
- Local interest. If you live in the area and have a dog, you might well be interested in the doughnut cafe
- Helpful. Ever tried giving a pill to a dog? Got a problem with your hamsters fighting?
- Star appeal. We all love to hear about someone who went viral right?

What's also surprising are the magazines that published these articles. *The Times*, *USA Today*—these are major publications and not necessarily the first ones I would have thought of when considering who might publish a pet-related article. *People* magazine—again, joining the dots between a celebrity magazine and pets might not be obvious, but if it's about a celebrity or a viral star—they are interested.

General interest magazines have a more varied audience—their readers are looking for a wide range of articles, not just one. This means that your idea needs to be compelling and interest their broad readership. So, consider how you could make your idea more appealing to a wider audience. Let's say I have an article about how to move home with a dog. Perhaps I could make this more appealing by changing the context slightly—how to make your next house move go more smoothly, even with a pet on board!

Option 3: Local Magazines

These may not have the gloss and glamour of major publications but they are a way of getting readership and getting your work published. You'll find these local publications in many places, and while they are very focused on their local communities, they need articles. They also like writers that are local and can be relied upon to provide quality content. It might seem obvious, but I'll spell it out—they want articles that have a local flavour. You're more likely to catch the editor's eye with a piece about vandalism at local dog parks than a general piece on dog parks.

You can find these magazines at a range of places—they may have their own websites but they might also have links from other sites. So try websites for your local communities.

Option 4: Trade Magazines

These are similar to a focused magazine but have a different audience—rather than people who buy products that are aimed at the people who will be selling them. They're interested in trends in the market, what people are interested in and new products—so you need to know your stuff and be well informed. An expert even!.

What Should You Submit to an Online Magazine?

Exactly what they ask for. No more and no less. Most online magazines will have a submissions page, if not try the Contact page on their website. Many sites want to know your idea first and will ask you to email them your idea - succintly, often in a specific number of words. Some magazines prefer entire articles sent on speculation. Your best bet is to check their submissions guidelines—if it's not on their website then do a search for submissions guidelines and the name of the publication. It's possible another writer has been kind enough to share their experiences of submitting to them. You can't necessarily rely on it (information online gets dated very quickly), but it's a start.

What's really important—and I can't stress this enough (I'm an editor, so I experience first-hand the time wasted by writers who don't bother to comply to guidelines)—you're far more likely to be noticed if you stick to their rules, than if you don't. Make a good impression and just maybe the editor will take a glance at your work. If they think you're going to be difficult or hard work, they just move on to the next submission.

You'll increase your chances of being accepted if your piece matches what they are after. Let's look at some examples.

This is from the submissions page of *Mslexia*, a magazine for women, that writes:

3

There are 17 ways to submit, from a four-line poem to a 3000-word lead article, from a 300-word bedtime story to a 700-word memoir performance piece—so there's bound to be something to suit your kind of writing. Including big-name commissions and as-yet-undiscovered newcomers, we publish over 60 women in every issue.

This is then from their pitch page:

Mslexia welcomes article and interview proposals—Journalism pitches for articles and interviews are welcome at any time. Send us a 200-word proposal, plus a brief CV and a published or unpublished example of your writing.

▶ https://mslexia.co.uk/submit-your-work/

Here's another from *Aurealis*, a Science Fiction/Fantasy online magazine:

Aurealis is looking for science fiction, fantasy or horror short stories between 2000 and 8000 words. All types of science fiction, fantasy and horror that are of a "speculative" nature will be considered, but we do not want stories that are derivative in nature, particularly those based on TV series. We do not publish horror without a supernatural element.

▶ https://aurealis.com.au/submissions/

As we can see from both of these examples, they are very specific about what they are seeking. *Mslexia* have provided a wide range of submission options and from their opening paragraph, I get a good feel of their style. If you've got an idea for, say an interview, they want to see a 200-word proposal—so that means don't send them the full piece. *Aurealis* is another example of a magazine with very specific requirements: You might have a great piece of horror but if there isn't a supernatural element, they don't want it.

How Much Will They Pay?

This varies greatly. General interest national magazines tend to pay better than local magazines but they are also much hard to break into and they probably look to see that you have an extensive portfolio.

Types of Magazine Articles

It's not quite as simple as writing your article and sending it off. Depending on the magazine, the format can differ greatly, so again (I know, I'm sounding like a broken record but it's important) you really do need to check their submission guidelines. It's important to identify if your article is a news piece or a feature article. Whereas a news article will report the facts and be shorter in length, a feature article will go into more detail. It tends to be more creative in style rather than just stating the facts, and will often provide more analysis and context. For example, a news report will give you the facts about a recent crime such as when and where it took place. A feature article about the same event might provide more information on recent crimes in the area, and go into more detail - such as investigating the people impacted.

Here are just a few of the formats you'll find:

- Lists. These work great online and are very popular with readers—you've probably come across them—title such as 10 places to enjoy the sunshine this weekend.
- Short paragraphs. Long paragraphs online just don't work. Online readers prefer it short and snappy and long stretches of text just aren't appealing.
- Sub-headings. Again, these work well online and the reader can quickly scan down to the part they are interested in. What? I hear you gasp—they won't read your entire piece? That's right, they probably won't. Just look at your own online reading habits and you'll likely discover you're the same as most online readers—you won't want to waste your time and scan to see if you actually want to read it.

Lists

Articles that contain lists are very popular online as they work extremely well with the way readers like to read online—it is easy to read on a small phone screen, the content is short and punchy, and the layout encourages your reader to keep going through your list.

Listverse is just one site that is devoted to the List format.
(► https://listverse.com/submit-a-list/)
This is from their submission page:

Before submitting your list make sure it is proof-read and edited. Lists that lack novelty are less likely to be accepted and all lists must conform to the highest standards of the English language. Lists that don't comply with our terms and conditions and our author's guide will be rejected without consideration. We only accept submissions from the US, UK, NZ, Ireland, Canada, Australia, and South Africa.

This is a website focused on fascinating and rare or uncommon facts. You can submit list posts that are 1500–2000 words long and, if successful, earn $100. Like all good websites, they want pieces that are proof-read and well edited. Your idea needs to be interesting, and in their words, novelty. Their guidelines ask for 10 items—and if you look at some of the articles they have published they contain 10 items. Not 9 or 11—so if they want 10, stick to it. They also want quality sources—so this means that you can't simply make things up. Your list needs to contain facts that are credible (and supported by sources).

You've Found a Magazine, What's Next?

Step 1: Review Their Copyright Terms

- Always, always check the terms and conditions of a site before submitting your piece.
- If you are accepted and agree to be published, this will be based on agreeing to their terms and conditions—so read them!

Some points to consider:
- Are you happy to transfer ownership, copyright, and other rights (such as moral rights) to the site owner?
- Some sites will retain the right to edit your piece—are you okay with this?
- Will your name be published with the article?
- You may be submitting your piece to a particular site but the terms and conditions may transfer all rights which means they can publish it anywhere.

Step 2: Check Submission Dates and Any Deadlines

In the case of *Raconteur Magazine*, they accept submissions at certain times of the year. When I was looking they helpfully stated at the top of their submissions page that they were open for submissions.

If it's a special edition, chances are there will be a specific deadline date that you must meet. Other sites will accept submissions at any time. But it's important to check.

On the website of *Black Fox Literary Magazine*, it explains that they publish a Summer Issue and then a Winter Issue, and have submission periods:
- Summer (2022) Issue Submission Period: March 2, 2022–May 31, 2022.
- Winter (2023) Issue Submission Period: September 1, 2022–November 30, 2022.

Step 3: Prepare Your Submission

When a magazine provides guidance for submissions, these aren't nice to haves—they are rules. They have taken the time to list these out for a reason. I am the editor for a journal and magazine and both receive many submissions. We have a small editorial team that cannot make significant changes to pieces. Often we have received so many submissions, that with tight deadlines, those that don't confirm are rejected. It might sound harsh but it also comes down to a publication having a consistent look and feel, and limited time to go back to writers to ask for revisions.

I've included a checklist at the end of this chapter which will give you an indication of the types of things you'll need to look out for.

❓ EXERCISE 3: Is It the Right Magazine?
Let's take a look at what *Reader's Digest* is after:
Your story must be true (no fiction, please). It should be previously unpublished. Aim for 800–1000 words in length. Familiarise yourself with the kind of pieces we run. Often, they focus on a single incident or theme in the life of the writer—dramatic, moving, or humorous—and the events described made the writer re-evaluate his or her life in some way. And remember that a well-told tale still has a beginning, middle, and an

end! Do not send us original or irreplaceable material. We cannot return submissions. We cannot give feedback or acknowledge receipt.

I've got some great articles I've been thinking of sending off. Do you think I should send the following to *Reader's Digest*:

1. The story of my grandmother's life. She was an amazing woman and I'm sure people would love to hear about her life. I'll struggle to fit it under 1000 words, but I reckon they'd still be interested regardless of length
2. My experience trekking in Nepal, where I visited a monastery
3. I once missed a train and was late for an interview. I didn't get the job so that late train was a life-changing event for me!
4. I've just taken in a rescue cat and I reckon everyone would love to hear about it
5. My friends and I recently went to a music festival and had an amazing time

- **CHECKLIST: Magazine Submission**

Abbreviations	Can you use abbreviations?
Overview	Some magazines like to have a brief explanation on what the article is about.
Biographical details	What do they want to know about the author? And how much word count do you have?
File format	The typical file formats for submitting are DOC, DOCX, and PDF. But sometimes they want something else, so you need to check. Make sure your Microsoft Word documents are not locked or protected. Some magazines have specific requirements. Their websites are the best place to check this and for any guidance.
Footnotes and endnotes	Do they prefer footnotes or endnotes or neither? Where should you include these?
Font and size	Check if they require a specific font and size. If they don't specify, stick to the standard fonts like Times New Roman, Times, Helvetica, and Arial. Never use fancy fonts—and stay away from Comic Sans—which just makes your piece difficult to read.
Formatting	Any special formatting they want or don't want? For example, some do not want to have tables or embedded images.
Headings	Check any requirements. Some places limit the number of heading levels, and make sure these are clearly indicated in the piece.
House style	This may or may not be specifically listed on their website but you can very quickly ascertain what this is by reading some of their accepted submissions.
Keywords	These are 3–5 words or phrases that succinctly and accurately describe your piece—and/or readers might use if they were searching online for an article just like yours.
Language	Check the languages that they accept. If it's English, do they want English or American English spelling?
Layout and spacing	Do they want single-spaced or double-spaced? Do they accept single or double columns?

3

Abbreviations	Can you use abbreviations?
Length	Check the length that is permitted (sometimes there are minimum and maximum lengths required)
Page numbers	Do they want page numbers? If so, how should they appear?
Punctuation	This might seem irrelevant but you try and produce a magazine with multiple submissions. All publications want to have a consistent look and feel, which means that all submissions must comply to their guidelines. Quotes are a good example—do they want single or double. Maybe they don't want spaces between page numbers.
Reference style	Which referencing style do they use?
Tables and figures	Should these be embedded or submitted separately? Captions? And any conventions for these?
Images	If images are to be submitted separately—what file types, dimensions, and size?

Publishing with Online Journals

Contents

© The Author(s), under exclusive license to Springer Nature Switzerland AG 2023
L. Kesteven, *Publishing Online for Writers*,
https://doi.org/10.1007/978-3-031-21366-3_4

About this Chapter

In this chapter we will:

- Consider how to find an appropriate online journal
- Discuss how to identify credible journals
- Outline the process for publishing with online journals
- EXERCISE: Write an Abstract
- CHECKLIST: Journal Submission Guidelines

4

Getting your work published online in a journal isn't as simple as it sounds. It is a competitive market, but when it comes to advancing your research and career, it's an important aspect.

Publishing in a journal is typically done by an academic who wants to increase the visibility of their work to others in their field of study. As an academic, we're keen to produce high quality research and add to our field. Getting this work published in a peer-reviewed journal is the logical next step to sharing your work but to also building up your reputation.

Unlike magazines, journals often have distribution networks—for example, their work can be placed in libraries and institutions, as well as emailing to readers and subscribers globally. I get new articles referred to me from Academia.edu, tandfonline, ResearchGate, and Common Ground Research Networks almost on a daily basis.

Why share your work? In addition to helping the writer build on their credibility, publishing in a journal enables them to participate in a community. Their research likely builds on the work of others, and hopefully interested readers may build on this in the future. This is why selecting the right journal is vital—if the article topic is going to be of interest and worthy of further discussion, then it needs to reach the right people.

But getting published in a journal is a highly competitive activity that can be very time-consuming and disheartening if things don't go well. Here are some steps to help the process:

Only Submit When Your Article/Paper Is Ready

While it's good to gain experience in submitting to journals, it's essential to first ascertain if your work is ready. Approaching journals before you're ready and receiving very credible, but all the same very disheartening, feedback, can be a harsh lesson. My advice is to seek feedback on your article from academics and other researchers that you know (such as from your own institution) before approaching journals. This will not only provide you feedback, but will give you an indication of how close your article is to being submitted to a journal.

Finding an Appropriate Journal

While there are likely less journals than magazines for an article, that doesn't make the process any easier. Again, there are journals for many and varied fields and areas of interest. It's very likely that as part of your research you've discovered the journals that have provided you with useful research and papers—that's a good indicator that they might be interested in your work. Ask your colleagues and other researchers in your field, the journals they find the most helpful.

Is the Journal Credible?

Here are some indicators that a journal is credible:
- If they are a credible journal in your field, then you should recognise them from your own research at least. Hopefully you recognise the publisher or at least the organisation they are affiliated with. Check their contact information.
- What are their affiliations? Who is on the editorial board? What about the authors they have published—are they experts in their fields?
- Does the journal have an ISSN?
- Do articles have DOIs?
- Is there a peer review process? Any credible journal will have this.

What Does Peer Review Mean?
This means that a board of scholarly reviewers in the subject area of the journal reviews any papers before accepting for submission. They will be checking for adherence to any editorial standards of the journal before articles are accepted for publication. This includes assessing the content for suitability as well as compliance to any requirements.

What Is a Blind Peer Review?
This means that the reviewers do not know who the author of the paper is.

Can I Find Out Who My Reviewers Were?
Probably not and it's not that important. If you feel that you have in some way been negatively impacted due to a reviewer, then the person to contact is the editor.
Other points to check:
- What is the journal's copyright policies?
- Do they charge a fee to publish your work?
- Are they Open Access?

What Is Open Access?

This is a set of principles and practices through which research outputs, such as journal articles, are distributed online, free of cost or other access barriers. If it's not open access, it means the publisher owns the rights to the articles in their journal and if you want to read the articles, you need to pay. Open Access means that research can be read by anyone without payment.

Is the Journal Indexed in a Database?

If a journal is indexed in a database it will be easier for others to find your paper. You might want to consider:

- Web of Science for journals spanning the humanities, social sciences, and STEM fields
- Scopus for journals in the social sciences and STEM fields
- SciFinder for journals in chemistry and related fields
- PubMed for life sciences, biomedical, clinical, and public/community health journals
- JSTOR for journals spanning the arts, humanities, social sciences, and sciences

Conferences and Journals

I've found conferences to be a useful way to link up with other academics. Over the years, I've attended conferences in my field in other countries—a great way to find out other approaches and challenges—as well as conferences in different fields but with a connection. For example, I presented at an art history conference that had a focus on the period of history I was writing about. I was fascinated by their findings and equally they were interested with what I was doing from a creative and fictional perspective.

Generally though, people who present at conferences also publish their work in journals. In the UK, the National Association of Writers in Education has an annual conference alongside their industry journal. With your sleuthing hat on, it's not difficult to research other academics and see where they are publishing their work.

In essence, find the right journal—they are extremely vigilant when it comes to selecting articles that fit their publication—so it's better to approach one journal that is a good fit rather than planning to approach multiple.

And while we're on the subject of approaching more than one journal, let's explore this further.

Should You Approach More Than One Journal?

You can, but it's best to stick to the principle of one journal at a time. This way you can get valuable feedback from one journal before approaching another. And it also avoids the embarrassment and potential copyright issues should two journals accept your piece. Also you might even find the same peer reviewer works for both journals (more even)—I do.

By all means, have a list of journals that look to be the right match, but approach them one at a time.

Understand the Journal's Aims, Scope, Guidelines, and Target Audience

As the editor of a peer-reviewed journal, I know all too well the importance of conforming to guidelines. While the font and layout might seem insignificant compared to the labour that went into the content—if you had to turn fifteen articles into one uniform journal publication, you'd think again. High quality journals have a consistent and professional look and feel that appeals to their readers and creates a uniform style across all of its content. Their guidelines will include many aspects from fonts, font size, how headings are used, figures, tables, page layout, quotes, and references. I've read that one article in five does not comply to requirements and are rejected on this basis alone, and I'd agree. If time permits and it's a quality article, I'll give the writer the opportunity to resubmit with a version that meets the guidelines, but sadly there isn't always the time available.

What Are Journals Looking for?

I took the following guidelines from the *TEXT* journal website. This is a journal that specialises in scholarly articles:

TEXT welcomes submission of research articles on creative and professional writing and processes, the teaching of writing and related issues. TEXT also welcomes the submission of creative work, book reviews, letters and notices providing that the matter of the creative work concerns exploration of creativity, or the nature and processes of writing, or the nature and processes of the teaching of writing, or investigation of writers' issues.

▶ https://textjournal.scholasticahq.com/for-authors

Here is another from the *Journal of Historical Fictions* and a Call for Submissions:

The Journal of Historical Fictions welcomes proposals from disciplines as diverse as archaeology, literature, film, history, media studies, art history, musicology, reception studies, and museum studies. We encourage ambitious approaches, using new methodologies to support research into larger trends, and more theoretically informed understandings of the mode across historical periods, cultures, media and languages.

Both of these journals have further guidance on their website with specific details on what they are looking for. Journals typically make the effort to explain what they are seeking—if they don't then move on—so take your time and really understand what it is they are after. You'll then be able to make the call whether you're a good match.

Dealing with Rejection

It's tough! Let's not pretend it isn't. Any kind of rejection, love, romance, writing, no matter, it's a tough one to take on the chin, and no matter how much we try to be resolute, it's not always easy to get up, dust ourselves off, and try again. Because of that, it's silly to put yourself through such an ordeal simply because you didn't comply to their guidelines—if you're going to be rejected, it should be for a good reason.

If a journal has taken the time to give you feedback, consider this a positive reflection. Not all journals will (not because they don't want to but because they often just don't have the time or resources). Feedback is part of your journey and learning about refining your work. If they give you an opportunity to revise your work, that's great, and take care to make the changes requested.

First Impressions Count

Would you go on a first date looking like you had been dragged backwards through a hedge? It must be tidy at the very least, no fancy ribbons or blowing kisses but presentable.

The title and abstract are an important part of your submission and they are the sections the journal editor sees first.

The title should summarise the main theme of the article and reflect your contribution to the theory.

The abstract should include the aim and scope of the study, the key problem addressed and theory, any method used, any data sets, key findings, limitations, and implications for theory and practice.

Edit, Edit, Edit

All journals need well-edited articles and have limited resources, so if you're thinking they'll simply fix your mistakes, then think again. They just don't have the time. If there's time, they might give you the opportunity to review a draft prior to publishing, but don't count on it. Most journals run to very tight schedules and there's a lot that needs to take place. Consider the peer review process alone—most journals are reliant on a team of reviewers who will read, assess, and provide feedback on submissions. Then there's an editorial process, graphic design and preparation for uploading onto publishing sites. In short, there isn't the time for writers to get their papers into shape. No matter how great the subject matter is, if it isn't publish-ready then sadly they'll move onto the next submission.

Many articles don't even get to peer review stage due to poor writing. It's not enough to edit your own work. We all become very familiar with our own work, and despite being diligent with your editing, it's very likely you'll miss some mistakes. But there are options.

Collaborate with others and you can review each other's work. You'll need to be prepared to return the favour and review other people's work and provide feedback, but I find it well worth the investment.

If you're really stuck, then you might want to consider using a professional editing company. It comes at a cost, but if you really want your article to be considered, it must be well written. A well-written, edited, and presented article projects a professional image that says you want your work to be taken seriously. On occasion, the major revisions conducted at the request of a reviewer will necessitate another round of editing.

Cover Letter

If a journal asks for a cover letter, then provide it. It's likely to be the first thing they read—and can be the decider as to whether they read on. So, take your time and craft it well.

A good cover letter:
- Outlines the main theme of the article
- Explains what's unique in the article
- Justifies the relevance of the manuscript to the journal
- One page is enough—any more and you risk the receiver not reading it
- Is succinct. There is no place for waffle in a cover letter
- Is professional. You may be witty and have a quirky sense of humour but the editor reading your cover letter may not

Reviewers' Comments

It's important to approach these with the right mind set. While it's tempting to burn them at dawn exclaiming 'they just didn't get it', take a deep breath and read them again after a few days (and you've had time to settle down).

I take my editorial role seriously and I appreciate all submissions, so even those that get rejected at an early stage receive an explanation why. It could be that it needs more editing or it's not suitable for the journal (too many fall into this category). I've had the rare instance where a writer has tried to argue the feedback. When an article has been peer reviewed, it means usually two or more reviewers have assessed the paper. The reviewers are usually experienced and know the journal's requirements well. If it's been rejected by the journal's peers then it's been rejected. Move on.

Sometimes reviewers accept with revision. This is good news and may include major or minor changes. It's important to address the revisions diligently and to address all comments raised.

❷ EXERCISE 4: Write an Abstract

Most journals will have a word limit for their abstracts so always check this. For the purposes of this exercise, try to write it to be between 250 and 300 words.

(It's very possible you're not at the submission stage yet and won't be able to answer all the questions, but it's always a good way to test if you article is focused and on track!)

Introduction	Keep it brief: What is the topic you are investigating?
Keywords	5–6 keywords that people would use to search for your paper.
Why is your chosen topic important to your field/s of study?	This explains the specific problem your research addresses. Identify your key claim or argument and the scope of your study.
What is the gap?	This is the gap in the research or literature and where your work fits in. (This isn't the background to your paper but is focused on your work.)
What is your research question/aims?	State clearly what your research problem is and the objectives.
Your research methods and approach?	If you're in a science field, include a summary of the methods that you used. If it's humanities, focus on the objectives of your research.
Key message	Succinctly say, in one sentence, the key message that you would like the reader to take away from your piece.
Summary of your findings	Summarise the most important results or findings.
Why your findings contribute to your field	This is your conclusion and explains to your reader why your findings are of value to your field.

▪ CHECKLIST: Journal Submission Guidelines

Abbreviations	Can you use abbreviations?
Abstract	Some submissions, especially for journals, need to have an abstract that briefly explains what the article is about. Again, it will have a specific word count.
Blinded submission	This means that they don't want to know who the author is. Therefore, any identifying information needs to be removed (and it's more than just the name). Sometimes details, such as affiliations, can identify someone.
Biographical details	What do they want to know about the author? And how much word count do you have?

File format	The typical file formats for submitting are DOC, DOCX, and PDF. But sometimes they want something else so you need to check. Make sure your Microsoft Word documents are not locked or protected. Some journals have specific requirements (e.g., some scientific journals want LaTeX manuscripts). Their websites are the best place to check this and for any guidance.
Footnotes and endnotes	Do they prefer footnotes or endnotes or neither?
Font and size	Check if they require a specific font and size. If they don't specify, stick to the standard fonts like Times New Roman, Times, Helvetica, and Arial. Never use fancy fonts—and stay away from Comic Sans—which just makes your piece difficult to read.
Formatting	Any special formatting they want or don't want? For example, some do not want to have tables or embedded images.
Headings	Check any requirements. Some places limit the number of heading levels, and make sure these are clearly indicated in the piece.
House style	This may or may not be specifically listed on their website but you can very quickly ascertain what this is by reading some of their previously accepted submissions (do your own research).
Keywords	These are 3–5 words or phrases that succinctly and accurately describe your piece—and or readers might use if they were searching online for an article just like yours.
Language	Check the languages that they accept. If it's English, do they want English or American English spelling?
Layout and spacing	Do they want single-spaced or double-spaced? Do they accept single or double columns?
Length	Check the length that is permitted (sometimes there are minimum and maximum lengths required).
Page numbers	Do they want page numbers? If so, how should they appear?
Punctuation	This might seem irrelevant but you try and produce an article with multiple submissions. All publications want to have a consistent look and feel, which means that all submissions must comply to their guidelines. Quotes are a good example—do they want single or double. Maybe they don't want spaces between page numbers.
Reference style	Which referencing style do they use?
Tables and figures	Should these be embedded or submitted separately? Captions? And any conventions for these? If images are to be submitted separately—what file types, dimensions, and size?
Title page	This generally includes items such as the author's name, any affiliations, email address, and contact details. But you need to check this as places will be different. Get it wrong on the first page and you'll make a bad impression.

Publishing via Blogs

Contents

© The Author(s), under exclusive license to Springer Nature Switzerland AG 2023
L. Kesteven, *Publishing Online for Writers*,
https://doi.org/10.1007/978-3-031-21366-3_5

About this Chapter

In this chapter, we will consider
- Should you be blogging
- What makes a blog great
- What do you want your blog to achieve
- Blogging platforms
- Pitfalls to avoid
- EXERCISE: Let's Explore some Blogs
- CHECKLIST: Producing a blog

5

Many writers have a blog and view it an important outlet for sharing their work. It gives them exposure and enables them to share their creative work as well as other related information, such as their creative process. But like any social media, it can be time-consuming; therefore, it's importance to be clear from the outset, what you want your blog to achieve. There are also writers who have blogs that sit there, like abandoned ships out at sea, forgotten and rarely seen—so before embarking on a blog, let's consider what it means and if it's right for you.

Should You Be Blogging?

According to WebTribunal: *In 2022, there are more than 600 million blogs out of 1.9 billion websites in the world. Their authors account for over 6 million blog posts daily, or over 2.5 billion annually.*
- ▶ https://webtribunal.net/blog/how-many-blogs/

Wow, that's a lot of blogs and as a reader, it's difficult to know where to start if you're looking for a quality blog to follow. Standing out from the crowd, when it comes to a blog, is only going to get more difficult, but let's consider what makes a blog one you're willing to read regularly:
- Relevant and regular content. That means it's unique, informative, newsworthy, and entertaining. If there are facts, these are cited and linked to credible sources.
- The blogger is knowledgeable, authoritative, and credible. Over time, their followers consider them an expert in their field.
- The blog posts have a recognisable style or 'personality'. Their followers enjoy reading their work.
- The blog posts are thought-provoking and inspire conversation. People love to share content and sharing a blog helps them connect to others.
- The content link up with other blogs—they don't stand alone but instead build a chain of information with other blogs.

So, first and foremost if you're considering whether to blog, you need to consider if you have:
- The time to devote to a regular blog.
- The knowledge to produce at least 12 blog posts (that's working on the premise of 1 blog post a week for 3 months) and have enough knowledge to come up with enough ideas to keep going.

- The resilience and motivation to keep going.
- A network that you can connect with and share links to other blogs. There are regular articles published online that review and recommend blogs. Network enough and have a good amount of readers/followers, and you might be lucky enough to be included.

What Does It Take to Be a Good Blogger?

If you're a writer, then that's a good starting point. Poorly written blogs don't attract viewers.

A good blogger wants to share their writing with a global audience and have a platform to share amazing thoughts and ideas. But the catch is delivering all of that on a regular basis. So, let's consider what it takes for a blogger to, not just be good, but be great.

Relevant Knowledge or Skill Set

Not only that, but they also need to have that magic that turns the boring and mundane into the extraordinary.

This is the blog for Dr Karl Kruszelnicki: ▶ https://drkarl.com/blog/

He describes himself on a university website as: *Karl Kruszelnicki used to be a 'proper pukka scientist, engineer and doctor', but is currently an author and science commentator on radio and TV.*

Take a look at his blog and you'll quickly see why he's so popular.

Provides Insights into a Topic or Industry   Do you need to be an expert? Not always, but experience definitely. You might just be a hobbyist, but if you've been through the experience, you can share that. Just be honest—if you portray yourself as an expert, readers will quickly realise that the so-called expertise might be pretty thin. You'll need to know enough about your particular blog topic to write regularly—so if your knowledge is only light, you'll need to start building it up.

Unique-ness   Plenty of people have become successful bloggers because they have a unique approach or style to a very familiar subject. Dr Karl above, has a very unique take on science topics and it has wide appeal. Perhaps you're a great chef—that's not unique and there are plenty of blogs already on cooking. But perhaps you're experienced at feeding a family of six on a budget of $50 a week.

Business Expertise   Business blogging is a lucrative form of content marketing that enables companies to engage with their consumers. Their blogs often provide their readers with added value. Let's say they sell bikes—no-one's going to be interested in a blog that constantly promotes their bikes. But if they have a regular blog which provides useful information on local places to go biking, tips on maintaining your bike, and useful bike accessories, then people are more likely to show an interest.

Engage Their Readers   Easier said than done. You can be an expert but if your writing doesn't immediately grab their attention, they'll just move on. Engaging is a craft—it's about content, it's about style, it's about relevance, it's about timing. Take a look at some great bloggers and try to identify what it is that makes them standout. This isn't about copying what they do. It's about understanding what readers like. Perhaps it's written in a humorous style, maybe they have a casual, friendly tone, but being able to identify what makes blogs unique will help you consider what you bring to your blog and how you can engage with your readers.

Work Ethics   Blogs need to be consistent and regular. If your readers are familiar with your weekly posts and they suddenly stop, they'll quickly move onto another blog site and are long gone. A blogger works to deadlines, just like most of us. And if you're blogging about cooking and then suddenly share your political views—well, as a reader, that wasn't what I signed up for. You didn't deliver on that virtual contract so I'm leaving.

Consistent Delivery   The blogging world isn't for one-trick ponies. Writing one brilliant post that captures attention is great but that following will soon disappear if you don't deliver the next time, and the next time, and the next time. If you find it hard to write on a regular basis, produce several posts at a time and then schedule them to be posting over a particular timeframe.

Self-Motivation   A blogger doesn't have a boss or an editor demanding that deadlines are met. The deadlines are still there—the writer just needs to be motivated to ensure they're met. This is an aspect that any freelancer can relate to, especially if you work from home and are not in an office. There are many distractions to call you away, but you need to focus on what needs to be done.

Be Different   What makes your blog differ from all the others out there? Be tough, stand back, and consider what makes you different from your competitors. Listen to your readership and what do they like? Give them more of what they like, and they'll keep coming back. While you might think you have the world's best idea, if it's not going to attract readers then you need to accept that something needs to change.

Know the Market   New blogs are coming along every day. And your readers are a fickle bunch. It's best to stay informed of what's out there otherwise you'll suddenly find all your readers have moved on to something new. So, if you're a blogger then you'll also need to be a regular blog reader as well.

Strong Writing Skills   If I spot poor grammar and spelling on a blog that's my cue to leave and I bet I'm not the only person. But there is so much more when it comes to making your writing top quality. There needs to be some craft and art—dare I say, eloquence, to the writing that appeals to the reader. It's much easier to spot than define, but it's those pieces of writing that are a joy to read.

Focus   Blogs that thrive support a community that have common interests. It's not just a blog for people who want to lose weight. It's a blog for people who are vegan, want to lose weight, are on a tight budget, and wear yellow jumpers (okay, I made that last one up). A niche helps give you that uniqueness.

Respect   Whether you're tackling pertinent issues or taking a casual approach to mundane issues, respect is key when it comes to your readership. Respect doesn't come automatically but needs to be earned by the writer—and that's achieved from credible information, supported by credible sources. That doesn't mean they'll always agree with you. Challenge is a good thing if it's done well. But if they don't respect you then you're just courting with danger.

Wisdom   Similar to respect but if you've done something and are sharing your experience—that's wisdom. Forget that image of the wise old sage sitting on a rock. You can be young and wise if you have experience in doing something. Reckon you can make it up with a bit of research on the web? That's a risky path to take and likely one that will quickly get exposed.

Passion   We're all drawn to people who are passionate about what they do or say. Enthusiasm is catching and done well, it's a great way to draw people in. Strong opinions are okay but bear in mind that others will have strong opinions too—and if you want to share yours, you can bet others will be just as keen to share theirs with you. So, best be prepared and back up your views with facts and cite sources. And be prepared to accept passionate responses.

Fresh Take on Something Old   Not always easy to do, but if done well, these can capture attention and give the reader something new to consider. As I'm writing this, there are so many issues going on in the world—and plenty of people wanting to share their views. I'm not so much interested in their views unless there is some credibility behind it. And that comes from their knowledge and the facts behind their views. Do I want to know someone's view on the war in the Ukraine if they're sitting in another country and are reading the same internet articles as I am? Not really. But if it's written by someone who has first-hand experience from the conflict, then you've caught my attention.

Thick Skin   Blogs are putting yourself out there and as much as there is admiration, you'll also find a lot of negative stuff. It's not nice and is a sad side of humanity, but if you enter the digital world, you're going to be confronted with it, whether you like it or not. Write an amazing article that people love, and you'll still attract negative comments—some will be completely unjustified, others just vitriolic and weird. Anonymity online makes it easy for hateful individuals to hide and be outright nasty without consequence. Reasoning will likely go nowhere other than to encourage more abuse, so best to ignore it and don't give them the pleasure of knowing they succeeded.

Networking Skills   Successful bloggers are great at networking and collaboration. If you're solely going to rely on readers coming across your blog, then your readership will remain small and limited. Forget worrying about competitive bloggers—these can become your collaborators and by working together you can drive traffic to each other's blogs.

Should You Have Your Own Blog?

You can, and it's definitely a great way to get your writing out there, as well as promoting yourself as a writer. But you can also write posts for other blogs (I"ll get to this shortly).

If you're going to have your own blog there are a few things to consider:
- You'll need to register for a domain name and hosting plan.
- You'll need to either build a website for your blog or use a blogging platform (such as Blogger, Wix, or Wordpress)
- Decide what your blog is going to be about. Having a niche means that readers will continue to come back to your site because they know you are an expert in a particular field. Or at least provide credible and interesting information on something. Yes, there are blogs about people's lives—but you need to have a particularly interesting life for people to want to come back.
- Remember, it's one thing to set up a blog, but it's another to keep it going. I know plenty of people who got all excited about having a blog and then ran out of steam.
- It is possible to make money from a blog via advertisement, sponsored posts, affiliate marketing, and selling products/services.

Getting the Blog Basics Right

A title is the headline that your reader first sees. So, it needs to reflect what your blog is about in a very few words. Keep it succinct. Test it on friends and see what their first impression is. If you must explain it, it's not working (you won't be there to explain it to your readers when they come across your blog online).

A blog is a visual platform and readers like visuals. Illustrations, pictures, diagrams—these all make a web page look appealing. Get it wrong and they can also make it look unattractive, cluttered, and migraine inducing. If you need to show a trend, the right graph can say much more than the written word—and your reader will quickly grasp your point. Select the right visuals and they will help reinforce your points, capture your reader's attention, and encourage them to keep reading.

Proofread your blog posts at least three times. A professional post has no mistakes—grammatical or spelling. Yes, we all make mistakes—and on the rare occasion we all forgive—but if you consistently write poorly then it screams unprofessional.

Writing Quality Blog Posts

Break Down Your Topic   Break your main topic into various subtopics and these are your headings for the post. This makes it easier to create longer blog posts and add content.

Make It Appealing   Think about what draws you to reading content online. Do you struggle to read long paragraphs of text and quickly move on? Most of us do. Content online needs to be short and snappy with gaps in between.

Your Content Must Be Credible   So, provide sources. This demonstrates that you have checked the facts you are stating and backing it up with sources. Readers appreciate this and can follow up the sources if they want to know more.

One Topic Per Post   If you have more to say, write further posts and link them together.

Have Something New and Interesting to Share   Not always easy to do. It might be a very topical subject that has been written about before but you have something new to add to the conversation.

Pitching to Other Blogs

Most online blogs want one of three things:
- A previously published blog post to feature (usually unpaid)
- An idea or pitch that the editor can give feedback on before writing begins (sometimes paid)
- A complete article unpublished anywhere else (sometimes paid)

You need to know what they want before you approach them. If they want an original unpublished work, then don't send them a post that's been published elsewhere. Other blogs will happily feature posts that are on your site already.

They'll be more likely to pay attention to your email if you know about their blog and have done your research. If you're sending out a stock standard email to numerous blogs which doesn't mention anything about their blog, don't be surprised if you don't get a lot of interest.

Blogging communities build up over time and they trust each other. If you want to work with other bloggers, you'll need to demonstrate that you've taken the time to get to know their blog, and that you have something of value for them.

Have a Niche

Or even better, have a sub niche. The more specific you can be, then you can really target your readership. You want your readers to consider you as an expert in your field.

Here are some examples:

Finance: Too broad. Are you focused on personal finance? Investing? Stocks? Cryptocurrency. And you can take it further. If it's about personal finance—who is your readership? A student trying to budget on limited funds? A young family? A professional eager to invest?

Do you need to be an expert to blog about such topics? That all depends—for example, if you're providing advice on what shares are good to invest in, then most definitely. If you're a student who has experienced first-hand how difficult it is to survive on a student loan, then you can share what you've learnt. You're not promoting yourself as an expert, but you're sharing your own experiences. Many people have done very well in such niches.

Travel: Again, it's too broad. But you could explore budget travel or luxury. Travelling on your own or in groups. Travelling as a family. Focus on a location or on a style of travelling (such as backpacking or cruises).

Fitness: Gosh, it's hard to know where to start. They are so many different forms of exercise, and then you can break this down into the different audiences. Then there is fitness for different groups (I'm thinking of people with different needs—e.g., those who enjoy running but have a knee injury).

Weight loss: Like the above, not everyone who is trying to lose weight are doing it for the same reasons or have the same goals. If you want to lose weight for health reasons is different than if it's more cosmetic.

Cooking: There are so many difference cuisines, different methods, different ingredients, different diets but again, narrow it down, such as vegan meals for a family on a budget.

Personal development: Motivation, self-improvement, career advice, coping with mental health issues. Again, if you can narrow it down, you'll appeal to a specific group.

The list above isn't aiming to show all the different areas—there are so many and I'm no expert to provide the definite lists—but what they show is that finding your niche takes time and effort. The more you can narrow down the focus, then the more a readership can relate to your blog.

What Is the Aim of Your Blog?

Unless you're happy with dabbling with blogging and taking a 'see how it goes' approach, having goals for your blog is a useful approach if you want to achieve a specific result. Here are some possible goals that you might want to consider:

Attract an Audience   If your blog is new, then you need to think about who your target audience is and how you will reach them. To do this you'll need to understand their behaviour—for example, what sites do they already visit? If there's an existing blog they visit, then having a link to your blog can help to drive traffic.

Who is your audience, questions:
- Who are they?
- What blogs or magazines do they read?
- Is there somewhere that this community is attracted to?

Answer Questions   Answering questions that your readership has is a great way to approach your blog. If you can find out the questions they have—and answer these—then it builds up your reputation.

On a similar vein, if you can find out the topics and conversations that are hot topics for the community, then you can contribute to an existing conversation. It might be adding to the topic or providing another perspective.

This is Really Important   I once had a student who wanted to write for the viewers of a very low brow, daytime television show. I eventually managed to get them to understand that if readers are watching very low brow, daytime television, they are unlikely to be reading Tolstoy (which was their style of writing). It was a lesson in writing for your audience and understanding what style and word choice would appeal to them. Getting to know your reader is very important to the platform you use to promote your work.

Promote a Product/Service   This will all depend on where you are at with your blog. I know a blogger who started out blogging about beauty products. She discovered a niche in affordable beauty products and as her readership grew, so did the interest from brands. They quickly realised that her promotion of their products was a good way for them to sell. What was great about this blogger was that she had some basic rules. One was that she always used the products. And two, she was honest. This built trust with her and her followers. She was also upfront with the companies that provided her with free products for trial—she made it very clear that her review would be honest and based on her own experience. She's still blogging today—and turning away some companies because they don't fit with her model—so it's worked for her. By sharing a personal experience with a product/service with your readership provides a personal touch and people tend to trust personal testimonials over advertisements.

Convince the Audience of Your Perspective   I follow blogs about conservation because it's a cause I believe in, and I want to know ideas for how I can treat our planet more kindly. What do I look for in such sites? I don't want to be preached to, but I like facts and ideas that have been tried and tested.

Share Important News   This might be global world issues or a local topic—but people like to stay informed. We don't have time to keep up to date on every subject, as much as we'd like to, so if there's a website that can keep us informed on subjects that are important to us—great!

Is Your Blog Hitting the Spot?

You'll only be able to tell if your blog is hitting the spot if you have clear goals that can be measured. If you want to build you audience then you'll need to know the number of visitors to your site and your followers.

If you want to make some form of income from your blog, then it's essential to take it seriously—and that means working out how much you need to generate from your blog to make it viable. This means understanding the traffic that visits your blog, how many followers you have, and monitoring trends.

Blogging Pitfalls to Avoid

- Forgetting your audience. Just because a topic interests you, don't automatically assume it will excite your audience.
- Writing too formal or stiff. Blog posts are a familiarity to them. They are nice to read—like talking to a friend. So, make sure your blog 'personality' shines through. Know your style and stick to it.
- Writing about you. Using your experience is good—but it's with a goal—you're using your experience to show a point. But remember it's not about you. If your blog becomes a personal platform it's likely your readers will lose interest (unless of course you're a celebrity—but they're probably too busy being famous to blog).
- Going off topic. Remember your readership decided to view the blog post because of the title so stick to that. Move off topic and they'll move on.
- Just repeating your opinion. Posts need content to be interesting.
- Posing a question without some answers.
- A post going nowhere. It's writing a-b-c but a post needs a beginning, a middle, and an end.
- A post forgotten. End your post with something memorable—perhaps it's an idea to consider or a question posed. If there's nothing memorable, your reader will forget the post (and likely the blog).
- What's the point? We've all read those meaningless posts where you end thinking, that was a waste of my time.
- I've read it before. If you've copied content from another source, then it's very likely someone will spot it. At a minimum, you've lost your credibility; at worst, you're accused of plagiarism. If you want to refer to someone else, do it properly—get their permission and cite their work.

Your Blog Is Organic and Not Set in Stone

Just because you published a post in the past, doesn't mean you should forget about it. The good thing about blog posting is that you can go back and update previous posts. If something has changed—revise it. Remember, for your blog visitors, they might be coming across a post that you published some time ago—it shouldn't feel like that to them, so keep it relevant.

? EXERCISE 5: Let's Explore Some Blogs

Find a blog to review or select one of these:

Zen habits: ► https://zenhabits.net/

Minimalist Baker: ► https://minimalistbaker.com/

Mr Money Mustache: ► https://www.mrmoneymustache.com/

My wife quit her job: ► https://mywifequitherjob.com/

The book Smugglers: ► https://www.thebooksmugglers.com/

Take 5 min to have a quick look at the website and then consider the following questions:

- What was your first impression?
- Did you find the blog aesthetically appealing?
- Was the topic of the blog immediately clear to you?
- Do they have a niche?
- Does the look and feel of the website suit the topic?
- Was there consistency between the blog posts?
- Who is their target audience?
- What's their style? Does it suit the topic?

- **CHECKLIST: Producing a Blog**

Objective/theme/focus of your blog	This can be broad and may change over time, but it will help when deciding on post ideas if you have a focus
What's your niche?	
Frequency	Weekly? fortnightly? monthly?
Target audience	
Blogging platform	Such as Wordpress, Blogger, Wix
Tone of blog	Think of five words that describe the tone of your blog: such as relaxed, friendly, casual, professional, vibrant

Ideas for ten possible blog posts. For each post ask: What's the point?	1
	2
	3
	4
	5
	6
	7
	8
	9
	10
Links to other social media?	

5

Publishing a Podcast

Contents

© The Author(s), under exclusive license to Springer Nature
Switzerland AG 2023
L. Kesteven, *Publishing Online for Writers*,
https://doi.org/10.1007/978-3-031-21366-3_6

About this Chapter

In this chapter we will:

- Consider podcasting and its place in the online publishing world
- Explore the podcast market
- Discuss how to make a podcast
- Reflect on how to take your podcast from good to great
- Brainstorm an idea for podcasting
- EXERCISES: (1) Exploring the World of Podcasts and (2) Promoting your Podcast
- CHECKLIST: Producing a Podcast other podcasts

According to Seth Godin (in late 2018), podcasting is the new blogging

▶ https://seths.blog/2018/10/podcasting-is-the-new-blogging-2/

And if we look at the statistics (from Insider Intelligence) then I'd have to agree with Seth Godin. In 2021, around 20% of internet users were listeners of podcasts and that is expected to grow to 23.5% by 2024.

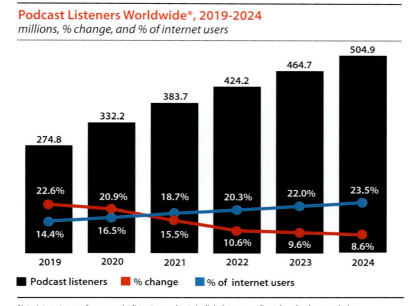

Podcast Listeners Worldwide*, 2019-2024
millions, % change, and % of internet users

	2019	2020	2021	2022	2023	2024
Podcast listeners	274.8	332.2	383.7	424.2	464.7	504.9
% change	22.6%	20.9%	18.7%	10.6%	9.6%	8.6%
% of internet users	14.4%	16.5%	15.5%	20.3%	22.0%	23.5%

Note: internet users of any age who listen to a podcast via digital stream or direct download on any device at least once per month; *includes Argentina, Australia, Brazil, Canada, China, Denmark, Finland, France, Germany, Italy, Japan, Mexico, Norway, South Korea, Spain, Sweden, UK, and US
Source: eMarketer, July 2021

269947   eMarketer | InsiderIntelligence.com

▶ https://www.insiderintelligence.com/insights/the-podcast-industry-report-statistics/

Here are some interesting statistics reported by Influencer Marketing Hub in 2022:

- There are over 2 million podcasts and 48 million episodes
- 78% of Americans are aware of podcasting. In 2006 this was just over 20%, so that's a big increase over 15 years
- 91% of Australians are aware of podcasting
- Podcast listening peaks in the morning
- Mobile phones are the preferred device to listen to a podcast
- Podcasting is growing more popular among older listeners
- 74% of podcasters use headphones while recording
- Podcast advertising revenues are expected to exceed $2 billion in 2023
- The demographics of podcast listeners are diversifying

▶ https://influencermarketinghub.com/podcast-statistics/

What Is a Podcast?

A podcast is an audio programme or spoken media, similar to talk radio or a radio show/drama. It is often a series of audio episodes, focused on a particular subject or with a theme. A podcast can be accessed via an app on your smartphone or laptop and you can listen to it whenever you like. You can also subscribe and be notified when new episodes are available. There are literally podcasts on every topic you could possibly think of.

But that's where the similarity to talk radio ends because it delivers much more. As a format, as well as being available to the listener whenever they want to listen to it, it offers a lot more flexibility:

- Podcasts can be any length. It could be a brief 1-min news item or as long as a 3-hour in-depth interview. The format and length are determined by the podcast creator as what will work best. Though there are statistics available on what works best for listeners and particular genres.
- Podcasts can be any frequency, from daily to monthly. They might run for a set period or continue for many years. Some have developed from an initial idea and have involved into an ongoing series with serious sponsorship.
- Podcasts can be any format, from a single show to multi-person audio dramas. The number of people can vary as can the format.
- Podcasts can be about anything and everything.
- Anyone can make and publish a podcast.

While there are video podcasts, most podcasts are audio only—and like radio—they are often listened to while doing something else. For example, you can drive, cook dinner, exercise, walk the dog, while listening. Most people listen to podcasts via headphones connect to their phones.

Is There a Standard Podcast Format?

Unlike radio where various formats became popular (such as the talk show), you will find some formats have become popular with podcast listeners. But the freedom that comes with podcasting means that it provides scope for experimentation.

Interviews, monologues, storytelling, and co-host conversation are some of the most popular podcast types you'll find. But you'll also find some experimental forms. While conversational podcasts might sound like friends having a chit chat, those that do it well will have a lot of preparation and planning behind it. We will explore some of the more popular formats at the end of this chapter.

Does There Need to Be a Theme to a Podcast?

Generally, there is a theme, but this can be range from very specific to very vague. There will generally be some kind of connection between episodes. For example, you can find many podcasts based on true crime stories—a good example is Bad Women: The Ripper Retold, which tells the stories of five women murdered by Jack the Ripper. But you can also find podcasts on a broad theme such as 'What makes you Happy' and each episode explores different ways to be happy.

When you're thinking about your theme, remember that listeners will connect to a podcast series because of something—they might get involved in the unfolding drama, they might want to learn more about a topic, or they like the approach and style of the presenters. The latter might explore many and varied topics but what is consistent is the presenters. So, if you don't have a theme, consider what will be that consistency that you provide your listeners.

Presenters?

This can vary. Some podcasts have a regular presenter or presenters, while some will have regulars who then interview different people each week. A lot of podcasts have a very simple premise which is like a few friends having a casual chat about something. Just like with other formats, such as radio programmes and TV shows, there is often someone who is the draw card. You will find very well-known people on podcasts. That doesn't mean that people who aren't famous can't present a podcast—it's been well proven that they can—but they need to be good at what they do and their style works with the podcast.

Professional or Basic?

A podcast can be very polished and professional—with theme music, sound effects, and professional editing. Others are produced in a cupboard in someone's bedroom using a smartphone and are very simple. Many have started out very simply on no budget and over time built up a following and then got funding through advertising or sponsorship, for example. But if you're recording your podcast using basic equipment, make sure you take extra steps to ensure the quality is as good as it can be. Recording in your living room with background noise probably isn't going to cut it (unless, of course, that's part of the show!). I've seen many a professional podcast produced by teams of students, who—through creativity and preparation—managed to deliver something that most listeners wouldn't have realised they didn't have professional equipment.

Making a Podcast

One of the huge benefits of creating a podcast is that you don't need to purchase podcasting equipment—that's not to say that you can't spend money on such things, and they will improve the production quality—but you can produce a professional sounding podcast with your laptop or phone, some recording software, and a small quiet space. While you can edit afterwards using various apps that are available (some for free), it's much easier and smoother if you get it right at the time of recording. Therefore, prepare your podcasts before you start recording and make sure you put a sign on your door while you're recording. Cutting out that interruption afterwards can be frustrating and time-consuming.

Your Recording Space

If you can rent a studio with recording equipment, great. But with a bit of creativity, you can create a suitable space. You might have laughed at my cupboard suggestion above, but it was a serious remark. If the cupboard is filled with hanging clothes then this is good for sound proofing as well as reducing echo and reverb. Though probably not great if you have a couple of presenters. You could also try a small room with plenty of furniture. Of course, the format of your podcast will influence your choice of space—if you're wanting to interview others, the cupboard idea isn't going to work!

Make sure there are no loud noises or chatter in the background. That said, if your podcast is interviewing people in the street, then you might want to have some low level street noise to give it atmosphere. There will always be exceptions.

Podcast Apps

There are various apps available, so I'd strongly recommend that you search what works best for you. Here are just a couple of suggestions:

Podcastle is an example of a free audio content creation platform that covers all the stages of podcast production.

Podbean, GarageBand, and Audacity are other free apps you might want to consider.

I'm not going to recommend any as it will depend on your requirements as to what would be best for you.

Audio Recording

Once you've decided on your app, then all you need to record your podcast episode is a laptop or a smartphone. A simple USB microphone setup can give great results if you choose the right mic. You're much better to get started and see whether you enjoy it before investing in audio equipment.

The Interview Format

Podcastle has a multi-track recording feature which is useful when you have numerous podcast participants. Your guests won't have to download any apps, instead they receive an invite link from you. At the end of podcast sessions, you will receive a separate track for each guest. This is also helpful when it comes to editing.

Editing

This takes time and effort—but a well-edited podcast is a must if you want to retain your listeners. While a small amount of banter can be engaging, a podcast that drags on with unnecessary waffle is frustrating for the listener, so edit away to keep it flowing and interesting.

There are podcast editing software that can help. Apps, such as Podcastle, GarageBand, and Audacity, have built-in editing tools which can assist with trimming and splitting your audio or performing more advanced editing such as removing unnecessary noise.

If you want to enhance your podcast, consider adding an opening tune or having podcast cover art (need some help to produce this? Take a look at Canva, an online graphic design platform).

Publishing

Some podcasts have their own dedicated website, which can help with generating traffic and give you a way to connect to your fan base, but it's not a necessity. You can publish your podcast by submitting it to a podcast hosting platform. There are many available—try looking at Apple Podcasts or Spotify.

The podcast host is the place where you save your audio files for further distribution and it provides access to storage space, web players, analytics, scheduling tools, and other useful features, making it easier to publish your podcast.

RSS Feeds (Really Simple Syndication)

Promoting your audio content via RSS feed is a way to keep your audience updated on new content. It provides your listeners with real-time updates on your content. Hosting platforms also provide you with your podcast RSS feeds, which you can use to submit to the directories of your choice. If you're not planning on using any hosting services, you can create a Podcast RSS feed.

Marketing

6

Once it's published, listeners need to find your podcast and want to listen to it. This is where your social media is invaluable! You can create a trailer to tell potential listeners about your podcast and provide regular updates via your social media.

If you weren't before, you'll have to get active on social media. Just like any product, it needs promotion, and social media is a way you can do this yourself with minimal to no costs, and reach out to potential listeners. But don't just tell them about the podcast—you need to sell it in such a way that people feel compelled to give it a try. Sometimes that's through a teaser, or by making the show sound so interesting they won't want to miss it.

- **Marketing via Your Network**

The internet is also the perfect place to enlarge your network and build exciting collaborations. Cross-promotions are beneficial for both sides. It can be fun cooperating with someone else, but each of you will be exposed to a new group of listeners that can help increase traffic.

Once your podcast gains popularity, you can join a podcast network. This is useful for several reasons. It can assist you with production and content distribution, but it can also give you ideas for making money from your podcast. When you join a network, your podcast becomes more accessible to advertisers. If you're lucky, you might find a company who thinks your podcast is ideal for their marketing campaign.

There are different types of podcast networks; however, all of them have entry requirements that include aspects such as revenue sharing, creative control, and mandatory collaborations. While you might be giving up a few things, you'll need to weigh up the benefits especially if you want to turn your podcast into a money-making proposition. Depending on your contract you might get funding, podcast sponsorships, and many opportunities for personal growth and development. Such networks also provide technical assistance such as free hosting service, your very own podcast producer, a dedicated website, and other marketing options.

Making Money

There are a number of ways to turn your podcast into a money-making operation—either directly or indirectly. You can sell the podcast itself or you can earn money from donations or creating premium episodes that listeners can access only after purchasing. Indirectly, you can promote other products or services and once you gain a relatively large following, you can find sponsors and advertising opportunities.

Taking Your Podcast from Good to Great

Research, Research, Research

Content is everything and a poorly prepared podcaster is obvious within the first few minutes. Even the best interviewers are prepared—they know their interviewee, the subject, and different topics they could explore depending on how the interview progresses.

An engaging interview reveals something to the listener that they didn't know before. So, hashing over old ground/old news just isn't going to cut it.

What qualifies as research? Just about everything:

- Why this theme/topic/subject? Put yourself in your potential listeners' shoes—why would they want to listen to this?
- Other podcasts—this will help you come up with something unique. If there are a multitude of podcasts available in your subject, you'll need to find a new angle to stand out.
- Other media—such as books, television shows, movies, magazines, internet articles.

The exercise at the end of this chapter considers some podcasts that have lasted the test of time and continue to be hugely popular. It's good to learn from these.

Preparation

Some of the best podcasts come across as very relaxed—an easy conversation between friends. Actually, what has gone on behind the scenes is very different. Give it a go and try and record a session with a friend with very little preparation—you'll very quickly see that they are gaps, too many ums and ahs, uncomfortable breaks, and conversations turning into waffle. Those podcasts that pull off the relaxed conversation well, do so because they've rehearsed in advance and are prepared for all (well most) eventualities!

Invisible Scripting

The intimate nature of podcasting is far more suited to being a conversation, as opposed to a sermon. Try to wean yourself off a fully scripted show with bullet points of everything you want to cover. This will become easier over time with practice, until eventually writing a full script will seem unnecessary.

Give Your Audience Something

Regularly listening to a podcast—especially a series—is a commitment, especially when some podcasts can run for an hour or more. So there needs to be something of value for your listener—that might be entertainment, but it can also include an element of learning or finding out something of interest.

Podcast listeners tend to be less committed than other formats. There are so many podcasts available, often people will listen to the first few minutes and if it doesn't hook them, they'll move on. It's very easy to just go and find another podcast. So, if your podcasts builds up slowly, you might find your listeners slipping away.

6

High Quality Audio

A Skype or phone interview will produce a low quality audio file and these just don't sound great. So make the effort—even if it's low budget—to produce the best quality audio you can. This doesn't mean expensive equipment, but you'll need to prepare and ensure your 'impromptu studio' is right.

The Podcast Host

This person can make or break a podcast and even if each episode includes a variety of guests, the constant is the host and their style. So chose your host carefully and make sure they're the right fit for your podcast. That might be you, but it doesn't have to be.

The Length

Anything from 20 up to 45 min seems to be within the 'sweet spot' for an episode length. How often? The best schedule is normally the most frequent one that you can stick to, on a regular basis.

Be Careful with Your Editing

Your podcast doesn't need to be perfect. Those mistakes, the words you pronounced wrongly, or the person's name you mispronounced, they can all add to the experience. But too many and it comes across as poorly produced. Long gaps, awkward pauses, and uninteresting waffle need to be removed so that what remains flows smoothly and continues to hold your audience's attention.

Getting Up Close and Personal

There's something very personal about the podcasting experience. You're listening to the person, you can't see them, and you're suddenly transported to a private space with them. In that closeness is the chance to get to know them more and understand the person behind the image. It's very possible that it's an ordinary person who has done something extraordinary.

It's quite an art to getting someone to open up—regardless of the media or environment—so practice your inter-personal skills and do your research. Listen and watch some of the people (doesn't have to be just from podcasts—consider TV and radio as well) who made their careers from interviewing. You'll see it's an art form in itself.

Experiment

With a low threshold to create and publish podcasts (anyone can create a basic podcast on their smartphone and then publish it), it's a format that lends itself well to experimentation. But it's important to remember that just because you've published a podcast, that doesn't mean that people are finding it. So if you really do want to test out an idea, it's important to also spend time on promoting and letting people know about it.

There are some great examples of podcasts that have grown into long-term series, while some have developed into other formats such as books and TV shows and movies.

Developing Your Podcast Idea

Step 1. What Is the Purpose of Your Podcast?

- Why do you want to make a podcast? Are you a freelancer? A business? For marketing purposes?
- Or are you looking at podcasting from a hobbyist's perspective? This might mean you'll be creating a show in your spare time. And the subject is something that you're passionate about.
- In either case, you can identify your 'why'. The why is important to remember. It keeps you focused and motivated, even when you're finding it difficult to get a show out.

Step 2. Who Is Your Audience?

- Unless you know exactly who you're making your show for, and why you're doing it, you've got no chance of finding and growing an audience. So, before you start writing your podcast, decide on your target audience.
- It's good to come at it from your audience's point of view—remember the— what's in it for them. For example, you might be a personal trainer who wants to make a health and fitness podcast. Your target audience might be people who are interested in healthy eating, weight loss, exercise, or bodybuilding. Do your research and see what's the hot topics at that moment. What can you add? Do you have an interesting angle on a well-discussed topic? It's essential to know, what's in it for your listener!
- If you're creating a hobby show—let's say it's based around your love of zombies and post-apocalyptic fiction—then your target audience would simply be folks with the same passion. They might be fans of TV shows like *The Walking Dead*, video games like *Resident Evil*, books like *World War Z*, and films like *Night of the Living Dead*. What's in it for them? They'll increase their knowledge of zombies and post-apolocalytic fiction and discover shows/films they might not know about.

Step 3. Choose Your Host

- It's possible you'll want to host yourself, but this doesn't always have to be the case. You can have a strong idea and bring in a host. While you might feel that it's your idea and you want to give it your personal touch by being the host, you need to be pragmatic and consider what works best for the podcast.
- What's important is to attract listeners with a distinctive voice, which will stand out amongst the many podcasts available. Listen to some podcasts and you'll quickly discover that some voice are just very easy on the ear.
- Listeners are on the lookout for something truly unique, so try to differentiate yourself from other hosts.

Step 4. Give Your Target Audience a Reason to Listen

- Whether you're providing information that will help someone to lose weight (in the case of our personal trainer) or conducting an entertaining interview with one of your favourite authors (in the case of our zombie podcaster), you're providing value for your listener.
- Not only have you given them a reason to listen, you have given them a reason to come back for more. It's important to think about this in the planning stages.

- Can you write down five potential episodes that you think your target audience would love to listen to? Do your research—and talk to people who you think might be interested—ask them what they would like to know or hear about. Better still, if you're building up an audience for your podcast, get them involved and ask them what they want. The more involved they are, the more likely they are to stick around and hear future podcasts in the series.

Step 5. Name Your Podcast

- A clever/catchy name is good—but don't get too clever! The podcast listener will quickly browse through titles and give yours a very quick glance. If it's not obvious what it's about, they might move on. Or worse, they'll think it's something that it's not and complain (loudly).
- A descriptive name—this helps. You want to attract your target audience so make it easy for them to find you.
- Your own name—this is good if people will recognise your name. If not … then it won't mean anything to the listener who's browsing for a podcast.
- Episode titles: Just like choosing a name for your podcast, choosing good, searchable, descriptive titles for your episodes is important.

Step 6: Choosing Your Podcast Format

The Solo Show

Also known as the monologue.

Benefits   You don't need to rely on anyone else to record your episodes, and you're building a reputation as the authority on your subject. The podcast is exclusively yours and you can make the calls on sponsorship and monetisation. And the profit is yours.

Challenges   Perhaps the most intimidating style of show for the beginner podcaster. One of the biggest challenges of the solo show is getting over the feeling that you're 'talking to yourself' and realising that you're actually talking to the listener.

The Co-Hosted Show

Presenting alongside a friend or colleague.

Benefits   This is a great way around 'mic fright' or dread of recording alone. It's basically chatting on the show with someone else. If you find the right co-host you have someone to bounce off, debate, or even mock (nicely). Some co-hosted podcasts have great chemistry between the presenters, adding to the listening experience.

Challenges   Not only do you need to set aside time to record, but that time must also be suitable for you and your co-host. There's also the question of ownership: whose podcast is it, do you split any future income 50/50? And what happens if your co-host loses interest or becomes unavailable in the future?

The Interview Show

This format is about 'Borrowing' the expertise or entertainment value of others. But don't underestimate the importance of the interviewer—it's not just about the questions they ask, but how they engage with the person they're talking to, and keep the interview flowing, such that it feels almost like sharing in a conversation between two friends.

In-person interviews versus over the phone: Given a podcast isn't a visual format, is it really that important to interview someone in person? Just like meeting in person, seeing someone enables you to read their body language and respond on visual cues. Personal rapport is established much more easily, and this comes through in your podcast. And you'll be able to understand the person better, ask more meaningful questions, and know when to change your approach because they're feeling uncomfortable. It's not always possible, but if you can, in person will give you a better result.

Who to Interview   Anyone who has an interesting story to share. They don't need to be famous—actually the best podcast interviews are those that come across as friends. It's casual and it feels like you're a part of a group of friends having a very natural and genuine chat. Sometimes it's the person less likely to be interviewed who has just an interesting story to tell—for example, while the person who came first in the triathlon at the Olympics will be bombarded with requests for interviews, the person who came second or even last can still have a story to tell—and it just might be fascinating. The best thing is, they might be more willing to speak with a podcast newbie!

Benefits   Talking to your heroes. Doing an interview show gives you the opportunity to have a chat with someone you've always looked up to. On top of this, your guests will have their own audiences who may listen to the interview and end up subscribing to your show. If done right, you can really grow an audience this way.

Challenges   Interviewing is a skill that you'll need to hone through practice, so don't approach the A-listers in your field straight away. You'll need to constantly find and approach potential guests, schedule interviews, and rely on others to show up (in person or digitally). Often, it's those interviews with the unexpected heroes, or the unknown people who find themselves in interesting situations, that can really draw a crowd.

Technology   You'll need to rely on technology (such as Skype or Facetime) to work properly throughout the interview, so make sure you have a test run with a friend before the actual interview.

Other Formats Roundtable—One regular host and several guests, talking through one specific topic
- Documentary—A narrator walks you through a range of interviews, conversations, and on-location clips to paint a picture
- Docu-Drama—A mix between drama and documentary. Offering learning and info, but in an entertaining way
- Fictional Story/Drama

Top Tips for Recording Your Podcast

- If using a microphone, watch your distance—too close and it can distort your voice. Be consistent with the position of your mouth relative to the microphone. If you drift away from the mic or even look away briefly, that will reflect directly in the sound quality of your episode.
- Grab your audience with your Intro and charm them with your Outro.
- Breaking your episode into segments makes it easier for your listeners to follow.
- Avoid too much fluff or waffle—this is the extra stuff people talk about that doesn't really have anything to do with the focus of your episode. A little banter is okay and can help engage your audience, but don't overdo it.
- Avoid over-editing.
- Be careful with editing if it's an interview or involves another person. You don't want to inadvertently change their meaning.
- Record some practice runs before the real thing and listen back to the recording. This will help you identify those small habits you might have that are impacting your recording.
- Have fun!

❓ EXERCISE 6.1: Exploring the World of Podcasts

Take a look at some of these podcasts worth looking at. You might not find the topic appealing but consider if from a production perspective. These have all become very popular with a strong fan base.

Lore:

This type of podcast centres around dark stories and mythology from history. Each topic is highly researched and told in a sombre tone with ominous music in the background. It's also become a TV show on Amazon Prime.

Welcome to Night Vale:

Welcome to Night Vale began in 2012 and is still going strong with two new episodes a month. The podcast is a fictional radio show that talks about the odd and supernatural occurrences in the terrifying town of Night Vale.

The Stuff You Should Know:

This began in 2008 with hosts Josh Clark and Charles W. 'Chuck' Bryant. They talk about things that the audience should know about in an educational yet fun and engaging style.

My Favorite Murder:

There are many podcasts devoted to true crime but this one has a comedic edge. Each episode the hosts, comedians Karen Kilgariff and Georgia Hardstark, choose a murder, a survivor story, or an historical event to discuss.

Films to Be Buried with Brett Goldstein:

Goldstein is a British comedian who interviews various celebrities and discusses films. The premise is simple, but the questions asked throughout, such as exploring why a film means something to the guest, prompt them to consider more about life, and death, than just the film.

My brother, My brother and Me:

With over 400 episodes, this podcast must be doing something right. It's described as a comedic advice podcast, but it's basically three brothers having some fun.

Listen to a few episodes and then consider the following questions:

- Would you keep listening?
- What did you enjoy about the podcast?
- Was there anything that you found grating or annoying?
- Was there anything that you noticed about the production quality?
- How different were the episodes? What was consistent between the episodes?
- What about the recording do you remember?
- What was the role of the host?
- How was the production?
- Is it an original concept?

❷ EXERCISE 6.2: Promoting Your Podcast

Write a short twitter post (no more than 80 words) to promote your podcast. Here's a few points to check if it's hitting the mark:

- Check the language you've used and does this match the podcast. For example, if the podcast is humorous then the post should reflect this. If your podcast is set in eighteenth-century England, then using contemporary language might jar (but not necessarily—all depends on approach!)
- Does it reveal enough to attract interest?
- Does it build intrigue?
- What's in it for the listener? Who is your ideal listener and would they be attracted to the podcast from this twitter post?
- Is there enough details for the listener to find your podcast?

■ **CHECKLIST: Producing a Podcast**

Objective/theme/focus of your podcast	This can be broad and may change over time, but it will help when deciding on editions if you have a focus
What's the audience's reason to listen?	
Frequency	Weekly? fortnightly? monthly?
Studio setting	Cupboard? room? hiring a studio?
Target audience	
Podcast format	Interview? Narrative? Co-host? Solo?
Tone of podcast	Think of five words that describe the tone of your podcast: that is, informative, casual, comical, hard-hitting, factual for example
Ideas for ten possible podcast sessions	1 2 3 4 5 6 7 8 9 10

Publishing
E-books

Contents

The E-book Publishing Process

Contents

© The Author(s), under exclusive license to Springer Nature Switzerland AG 2023
L. Kesteven, *Publishing Online for Writers*,
https://doi.org/10.1007/978-3-031-21366-3_7

About this Chapter

In this chapter we will:

- Consider how you know you are ready to publish
- Cover editing, feedback, and refining
- Discuss the stages of online publishing
- How to plan your e-book project
- Reflect on how you are the Project Manager not Jack-of-all-trades when it comes to publishing an e-book!
- CHECKLIST: Online Publishing To Do List
- EXERCISES: (1) Free E-books and (2) Investigating Self-Publishing Companies

This chapter covers the various stages to take a book from being written through to getting published online. Before embarking on the process, I will first cover how an author can assess if their work is ready for publishing. It's important to plan out what needs to be done and with a budget identified, decide those activities the author can do themselves, and those where it would be better to engage an expert.

What Is an E-book?

Similar to a printed book, an e-book (short for electronic book) delivers information in a digital, long-form publication. An e-book uses either a computer, mobile device, or e-book reader to display the content and can have multiple digital 'pages' to navigate through.

When to Decide If You're Going Down the E-book Path

Do you need to decide up front, before you have even put pen to paper (or fingers to keyboard) that you want your work to be published online and that it is going to be an e-book? Definitely not.

Some writers focus on writing first and then decide how to publish, and that's absolutely fine. Especially as we might want to 'test the water' first with one publishing approach, such as going down the path of having an agent who finds you a publisher, and then change to another. Or you might want to do both.

There are some very well-known books that you might be surprised to hear began as an e-book. *The Martian*, by Andy Weir, is one example and after being self-published it didn't go to print but was picked up by a small Canadian audiobook company. So, if you think of self-publishing as a 'last resort' because you weren't successful finding a traditional agent and publisher, then think again. There have been many examples of successful authors who have found publishing online worked for them, and plenty more examples of authors who publish both online and in print.

However, there are some benefits associated with knowing the path you'd like to take. While a novel can easily be published as both in print and online, it's not the same if you're producing a non-fiction or children's book where use of colours and images, for example, will be impacted by the final format.

Use of Images, Charts, and Diagrams

You might think this is not so relevant if it is a novel but there are instances where you might want to include images or diagrams. For example, if your story has a large cast, it can be helpful to include family trees. And if it is a fantasy world, a map might come in handy for the reader. When I wrote my first historical fiction novel, I wanted to include images from the period, but of course when it came to publishing it in traditional print format, it was just too expensive, and they had to go.

► Example

Where an image helps the reader engage with the narrative:

≡:   **The Ruby Brooch (Time Travel Romance) (The Celti...**

Aa

US Department of the Interior Bureau of Land Management

■ (From *The Ruby Brooch*, by Katherine Lowry Logan)

≡:   **Master of Furies: Epic conclusion to the Sunday...**

Aa

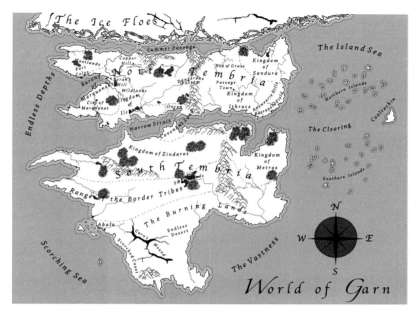

◘ (From *Masters of Furies*, by Raymond E. Feist)
◄

Where images and illustrations really can make a difference is if you are writing a graphic novel, non-fiction book, or a children's picture book. Printing glossy, high quality images are expensive if it is going to be physically printed. But if it is online, that cost no longer exists. Limitations on the number of images that would apply in the traditional print world are gone out the window, and you can go to town with imagery (though I'd strongly advise that you do so only if it will benefit your work). Overdo it and your reader won't thank you.

Key E-Book Decisions

Benefits of Deciding Up Front It Is Going to Be an E-book

You might want to link to other online content. Let's say you are writing a self-help book and you want to link to resources that are available online at other sources or say your own blog. If you are going down the traditional print path, then the only option really is to list the links in your content (and hope they don't change). However, if it is an e-book you have in mind, then these links can be active.

Maybe you'd like your publication to be more dynamic and have regular updates. This is not something you can do easily with a printed publication, where any reprints take time, resources, and money to produce. However, if it is an e-publication, you are in the command seat. Not that I am advocating having to fix typos and mistakes you find in your work—they should not be there in the first place. But there are instances where it is important to keep your e-publication up to date. Let's say you refer to the latest statistics. If it is an e-book, you can ensure your work reflects the latest figures and doesn't quickly become outdated.

Does Your Genre Affect Your Decision?

Potentially. For example, some genres sell better than others as e-books, so it is worth doing your research and seeing if indeed your genre has a strong following online.

Some popular genres selling well as e-books:

- Romance: It's not so surprising that romance has been the top-selling e-book genre for decades. There are also many sub-genres, contemporary and historical just two examples.
- Crime and Thriller: This is another popular e-book genre, often published as a series (such as with the same detective solving different mysteries).
- Fantasy and Sci-fi: A very popular genre online, these often build up a loyal audience base and offer additional books by way of a series, keeping their readership hooked.
- Self-help: These types of books have a huge following, both as e-books and as printed copies.

Niche genres: You work might fit into a very niche genre with a limited but niche audience. And it's very possible that niche audience has a community online that you can connect with.

Does the Target Audience Affect Your Decision?

Statistics show (from Statista) that some age groups are more drawn to reading e-books than others. It's probably not surprising that the 18–25 is the group most inclined to read an e-book (though often on a smart device rather than an e-reader). Some countries, such as Germany, prefer printed books whereas others, such as China, are avid e-readers (from Statista). In America (according to YouGovAmerica) more women read via e-readers than men.

Is It One Book or a Series?

This is where e-books work differently to traditional books. That's not to say that traditional books don't have series—they do, but the time between the release of the next in the series is much longer with traditional books. This is where e-books have the edge. I know an e-book writer who writes full-time and releases a new e-book in her series every 2 months. That's some commitment to writing, but over time she's built up a fan base and it has turned her writing into a profitable proposition.

Whether to produce one book or have it as a series is an important decision. The benefits of a series? It allows you to test the market initially with something shorter. If it gets interest and people are beginning to read your work and they like it, they'll want to purchase the next one. Knowing it will only be a short period of time before it is released is a huge bonus. Or if they have discovered your work once you have published numerous books in the series, the reader can continue reading on after the first. One of the benefits readers highlight with e-books is that they can become engrossed in a series, and they can keep reading with regular releases of the next instalment not too far away.

Length of Work?

E-books tend to do better if they are not too long (if it is going to be long, you might want to consider turning it into a series). Your typical online reader doesn't tend to read for hours in front of a screen, and they tend to choose shorter e-books for that reason.

Could It Be Part of a Package?

If it is a novel, you might be able to try marketing it as part of a package. For example, you might be able to offer your readers additional content available via a website. If its non-fiction, readers love added extras. For example, if it is an e-book on nutrition and eating well, you might include links to your blog where you regularly post recipes. Maybe your e-book is on teaching particular skills—perhaps you could have additional training material available? It's all about giving your readers added value.

What we are talking about here is turning your e-book into something more. A complete offering. This is an appealing proposition for readers as it is providing value add over what they might get if they purchased something similar in print form.

Is E-publishing for You?

Do you have the skills to self-publish? By this, I generally mean project management. You don't need to be a graphic designer (you can engage the services of a freelancer to do this for you), an illustrator (again, this is a service you can hire), or a marketing expert (most of the platforms have advice and offer standard packages), or even an editor (you can engage a professional). You do, however, need to be well organised and be able to plan.

Do you have the time to self-publish? I've noticed a trend with the writers who typically do well online—and it's that they make a career of it, even if it's not their full-time job (which for many it isn't). They are prepared to put in the time and effort to promote the work, weekends, evenings, regular hours, not piecemeal when they can be bothered but just as they would if it was an evening or weekend work. And it is time-consuming. You might have all the will in the world, but if you don't have the time, it's not going to sell in any significant volume. Do you have 2 hours a day, 7 days a week? Your e-book might be published online, but it won't be attracting anyone's attention unless you dedicate time to it.

Maybe you are not planning on selling your work widely. It might be a project that you want to only share with your family and friends—such as writing a family memoir—so your objective is to have your e-book available online where they can access it.

Perhaps you've done your research and you can see similar publications (same genre perhaps) are performing well online. That's a great indicator that your target audience are online readers.

Why Create an E-book

It's possible you've written your book and want it published, but it's also possible you have content in a variety of places (let's say you're a blogger). E-books can provide some advantages to a range of content creators:

- Compared to in-print publications that need to be physically printed and shipped to a store or reader, an e-book is available immediately—let's say I can't sleep at night and want to read something new at midnight. This is when your online bookstore has real advantages.
- An e-book provides you a way to collate your information in a useable format for the reader. The content you're reading in this publication was originally produced for a range of different sources—for a university module, for a blog, for students, for papers. By pulling it all together into one publication, it's much more useful to someone who wants to work through it on their own.
- Value adding; an e-book allows you to provide further information—that might be additional in-depth details, exercises, images—that you cannot include elsewhere.
- After the initial investment to create the e-book, it can be distributed endless times without additional production costs.
- No shipping fees or waiting times.
- Include links to other media and content.
- You're giving the reader options—some love their printed publications, others prefer to have it on their e-reader.
- E-books are accessible—the reader can decide the size of the font, the font, and there is also the option of text-to-speech so it can be read out loud to the reader.
- Build brand (as an author, YOU are the brand) awareness and establish brand authority.
- Expand your readership reach and gain trust from your audience.
- Provide your readers with valuable content, building trust in you as an expert.

- Generate interest in your work in general (not just the e-book) but it can encourage growth in other areas, such as other books/e-books and blogs.
- Extra income source—more readers equal more income.

Can You Make Money from Your E-book?

That all depends on the volume you sell. E-books tend to be high volume and low price, meaning you need to sell more. However, if you consider the reduced production costs, and if you're self-publishing you're not having to share those profits, so if you sell enough, then you can make money from your e-book. What does it cost to set up your e-book? I'll come to that later in this section, but the rarer and more popular your publication is, potentially the more you can charge. But just like any book, printing or online, its success will largely be determined by its popularity.

Steps of the E-book Publishing Process

1. Format your book for e-publishing
2. Produce a Design Brief
3. Design a Cover
4. Decide on your Publishing Platform
5. Upload your files
6. Produce your Marketing Strategy
7. Start Selling

Do you have to do all these steps yourself? No, you don't.

If you are an indie author then you will be responsible for all these steps and ensuring they happen, but you might not do everything yourself. Think of yourself as the person who oversees or manages what happens when—they might do some or all the activities themselves, but they can also get help where it's needed. The cover is a good example of this and is an area that you don't want to get wrong. The cover is often the first thing that screams out 'I'm self-published'. If you are an indie author and you have graphic design skills, you can give it a go, but seek feedback from sources you trust. Remember, graphic design skills aren't all you'll need—you'll also need to understand what makes a good design. There are applications available that have templates you can use (we will cover this in a later chapter). But if you are unsure and you have the budget, engaging a freelancer to design your cover is probably not money wasted. Images are another example of this. Consider children's picture books where the imagery is just as important as the text—if you're not an artist, outsourcing this to someone else makes a lot of sense.

Now, you might want to be self-published, but the list above may seem a bit daunting—and if it is your first time publishing online, that would not be surprising. But there is help available via several sources. Many of the publishing platforms, such as Amazon, have extensive help resources available to assist. But if you'd like someone to look after this for you, then you can buy these services via a self-publishing company.

The best advice I can give is to be prepared and manage the process. By producing a plan before you start writing, it will help you understand the work involved and the amount of time you need. It's not complicated but there are various steps you need to do, to be prepared for the next stage. For example, ensuring your manuscript is in the right file format. It's not difficult but it can be time-consuming. But with preparation and management and following a step-by-step process which I'll take you through in this Part of the book, the daunting aspect quickly disappears!

7

What's a Self-Publishing Company?

Basically, these are companies that help you self-publish. You are still effectively self-publishing, but they do all the hard work for you—at a price. If you have never self-published before, you might want to consider going down this path. It is a way of learning how it works and having someone to hold your hand as you do so. The downside? It will cost you. Prices vary depending on the service, so I strongly recommend you compare a few companies before committing.

A word of warning: When you send your work in to these companies they will probably give your ego a long overdue boost. They will tell you they can see merit in your work and that they would love to publish it. I am not saying there isn't merit in your work, but be wary that they want your business, and like publishing platforms, it does not harm their reputation if your book is not selling. Their business is in making money helping people to self-publish, so unless it is very poorly written, it is in their interest to take your manuscript (and money).

These companies often provide additional services, such as producing printed versions and marketing packages. They certainly take the hard work out of self-publishing, and if your budget can afford it, it is worth investigating.

Is Your E-book Ready?

In the traditional publishing world, when a writer is getting ready to send off a precious manuscript to a potential agent, they will generally stress and strain over getting it as clean and error-free as possible. It is no different in the online world—only it might seem so because you can effectively publish ANYTHING online without having it checked over. It might be filled with shocking typos and grammatical errors, but would Amazon or any other publishing platform care? Not one bit.

Have a quick look on Amazon and see how long it takes for you to find an obvious self-published book. The cover is sometimes an obvious giveaway. You might be thinking, isn't this sloppy of the platform not to care? Well, from their perspective, it is the writer's reputation that's suffering, not theirs. And unlike a physical bookstore where shelf space costs money, online that's not the case.

So, if you are going down the online publishing route, it is up to YOU to ensure your work is well edited. Traditionally, your agent would usually get your work reviewed by an editor, so it is a clean copy that goes off to print. Remember with online publishing, the writer is in the driving seat which means YOU must ensure it is well edited.

Can you do this yourself? It is an option, but you really need top-notch editing skills, and it is not easy when you are editing your own work. At a minimum, I recommend finding another writer who you trust who can go through your manuscript (in my experience, if you can find other writers who are willing to collaborate, you can often help each other and edit each other's work). If you can stretch your budget, paying for editorial services is certainly money well spent. A quick search online will typically return a good number of editors—do your research and compare. And don't ignore the online community—sites such as **Reedsy** [▶ https://reedsy.com] will often connect freelancers together. Here you can find a marketplace where you can find editors, graphic designers, and so on selling their services.

And of course, don't ignore free online apps such as **Grammarly** [▶ http://Grammarly.com] which can detect errors. If you are going to engage an editor, it is best not to spend your money on them picking up basic mistakes you can identify yourself, but for them to provide feedback on improving your writing and the story itself.

Planning for Publishing Your E-book Online

The plan for publishing your e-book does not need to be complicated or lengthy, but understanding what is required by when, will help you identify the time required and any support services you might need to engage ahead of time before you need their services. A simple table in Microsoft Excel will do the job (listing task, who is responsible, the number of hours/days to complete, and by when) or there are useful apps available which take a lot of the hard work out of managing a project plan. The checklist below will get you started.

Online Publishing to-do List

Task	Who	By when
Manuscript is complete	Self	
Have manuscript copyedited and proofread	Self or outsourced	
Is online published a viable option for your work?	Self	
Produce a Design Brief	Self	
Design Cover	Self or outsourced	

Task	Who	By when
Write blurb	Self	
Decide on publishing platform or self-publishing company	Self	
Create files as appropriate for your chosen platform/s	Self or outsourced	
Upload files or email files (if using a self-publishing company)	Self	
Obtain ISBN number	Self or outsourced	

Have You Read Material on an E-book Reader?

7

If you haven't, then this is the first thing on your to-do list. Getting your work successfully published online (and by this, I mean sold AND read by readers) requires an appreciation of the experience and how your piece will translate digitally.

E-books can be read in a variety of ways. Readers might use:

- A dedicated e-reader (such as the Kindle). Some of the latest e-readers have 'electronic ink' technology that comes close to reproducing the appearance of printed text on paper pages. Kindle's Paperwhite is an example of this.
- Multi-purpose tablet devices (such as an iPad).
- Smart phones and other mobile devices.
- Several different devices over time, picking up where they left off (e.g., using a Kindle Paperwhite at home and a smart phone on the train).

If going down the path of using a multi-purpose device, such as a phone or tablet, the reader will need to download an e-reader application. Some of these include:

- Kindle App. This is a free e-reader that allows you to read e-books purchased from Amazon.
- E-book Reader. This application can read several different types of e-book files including e-pub and PDF files.
- Kobo (anagram of 'book') e-Books. The original version was released in May 2010. It was marketed as a minimalist alternative to the more expensive e-book readers available at the time.
- Google Play Books. Play Books, like e-Reader and Kobo Books, reads several different types of e-book files as well as hosting millions of their own titles available to purchase in the app.
- Overdrive. Used by many libraries to offer e-book borrowing to their members. If your library has e-books as part of their catalogue, they may use Overdrive to access them.

Choosing an E-reader

While you don't need to have an e-reader to publish your e-book, it certainly helps a writer to see how their work will appear and experience e-reading first hand. I personally send my manuscripts to my e-reader as it's a great way to proofread and spot errors. Just seeing a manuscript via a different format is a way to identify mistakes that you might otherwise overlook.

I'm going to deviate for a moment and discuss aspects to consider when choosing an e-reader:

E-Ink Versus LCD Screens   LCD screens generally come on e-readers that have more functionality than just reading. However, they are backlit which can be hard on the eyes long term. E-Ink is the top-of-the-line screen types and they are designed to mimic a paper-like reading experience and are easier on the eyes. Almost all the Kindle devices are e-Ink.

Buttons Versus Touchscreens   E-readers come with three primary interfaces. They are either button controlled, touchscreen, or both. Touchscreens are popular and easy to use, while some cheaper e-readers still contain buttons for control. Some e-readers tend to use both the button and the touchscreen experience. The buttons control the power supply, and the touchscreen allows you to flip through books with ease.

Size and Weight   E-readers come in a variety of sizes and if you want to put your e-reader in a case, you'll also need to take this into consideration. Depending on where you'll use it most—maybe you'll want to fit it into your bag so you can read it on the train, or you'll be mostly reading in bed at night—will influence your choice on size.

Battery Life   E-reader typically has a longer battery life than your standard tablet with the average reader lasting up to 4 weeks with regular usage. But this will vary depending on how avid a reader you are. Some devices are better than others—for example, the Kindle Paperwhite can last up to 6 weeks on a single charge.

Waterproofing   There are waterproof e-readers available, which can be useful if you want to read by the pool, at the beach, or in the bath.

Anti-fingerprinting   One of the downsides of a touchscreen e-reader are the fingerprints left behind. Having a screen that doesn't allow for fingerprints resolves this problem.

Highlight and Note   This is a great feature for proofreading and allows you to make notes as you are reading.

Paperwhite   These e-readers make it easier to see the screen when it is sunny or in the dark, without straining your eyes.

E-books and Genres

Perhaps unsurprisingly, certain genres are more popular as e-books than others. Children's e-books have had a decline in sales—perhaps not so surprising if parents are hesitant to give young children access to electronic devices. Other genres sell better online than in print. Science fiction and fantasy fall into this category, as do romance, mystery, and horror. There is one genre that has done extremely well online, taking approx. 75% share of the market—and that's adult fiction. I guess it is not so hard to wonder why that might be. Read a physical book on a train and everyone knows what you are reading. But if it is on an e-reader, no one has a clue.

An Indie Author or a Self-Published Author: What's the Difference?

Simply put, a self-published author is someone who has published a book online. An indie author has also published a book online, but they also do a lot more.

According to the Alliance of Independent Authors
(► https://www.allianceindependentauthors.org/), an Indie author is someone who:

- Maintains complete creative control over their e-book and the publishing process.
- Is an author who has self-published at least one book.
- Doesn't necessarily do everything themselves, but they remain the person in charge. They may purchase services from others (like a construction project manager will oversee the building of a house, but they outsource the tiling to a professional tiler).
- Views themselves as the creative director of their e-book/s, from concept to completion and beyond.
- Doesn't seek to be published by traditional publishers. They're not looking for the validation some might perceive with being published by a traditional publisher. They take their validation, and mark of success, in the number of readers buying their book/s.
- Make partnerships that help deliver the best possible book to the most possible readers, trade publishers included. Sometimes that might well involve working with an agent to sell certain rights, or directly with a trade publisher.

What's the Difference with Self-Publishing?

A self-published author is anyone who has a self-published book. However, where it differs from the indie author is that they get someone else to look after the online publishing process for them. For example, they might purchase a package from a self-publishing company that includes a range of services a self-publishing author needs. Their packages often include the basics, including ISBN, copyright, designing/formatting, printing, listing with retail sites. Everything else can be bought at an extra cost, such as marketing materials, editing, proofing, distribution, and so on.

Of course, everything comes at a cost and this route adds another business/es into the process, which costs more money. Using such a service is likely to mean royalties equal slim to none.

Why might you go down this path? These companies take the hard work out of publishing your work online, and if you haven't done it before, they can do it all for you—at a cost. For a first-time author, this route allows you to learn the process of self-publishing and discover what you are capable of as well. Some authors don't have the time and/or skills to manage the online publishing process themselves and would rather focus on their writing. If you have the budget and don't have the time or skills, then they are definitely a viable option.

Just be wary of companies, or going with options, that only get your work published online and do nothing more. This is okay if you're not interested in selling your work (e.g., maybe you've written a story about your family and it's for a very limited distribution) but if you do want to sell your work then getting it online is just the first step.

Remember   These companies are making money by publishing books online—it might sound harsh, but their business model isn't about whether your book sells or not. Therefore, when you send your work to these companies, they will often reply with great enthusiasm about your work. If you've been down the traditional route of approaching literary agents, their enthusiasm and praise for your work can feel amazing. But don't forget this is a business transaction. Read the contract well and understand exactly what services they are providing and know what you'll need to do yourself.

❷ EXERCISE 7.1: Free E-books

There are sites available offering free e-books, such as Project Gutenberg. Project Gutenberg is an online library of over 60,000 free e-books (available at ▶ Gutenberg. org).

The first e-book was created on July 4, 1971, by the founder of Project Gutenberg, Michael S. Hart. It provides free e-pub and Kindle e-books, for download or to read online. It provides some of the world's great literature, with focus on older works with expired copyright.

If you are going to fully appreciate the online experience of e-books then you need to go through the experience of finding, downloading, and reading one. So go onto Project Gutenberg and find a book you'd like to read.

Now the next stage is important. Whether you use an e-reader, your smartphone, your computer, or a tablet, you need to experience reading online. It doesn't need to be the entire book, just a chapter is fine, but before you can truly appreciate e-publishing, you need to understand the e-reading experience.

❓ EXERCISE 7.2: Investigating Self-Publishing Companies

Here are six self-publishing companies. There are many more out there, but for the purposes of this exercise, I have selected a handful. I am not advocating any of these companies—what works for one writer will be different for another. So, if you want to select a company, you need to compare, which is what you are about to do now. Select 2 or 3 and compare the services they offer:

1. Kindle Direct Publishing: ▶ https://kdp.amazon.com
2. Barnes and Noble Press: ▶ https://barkerandjules.com
3. Draft2Digital ▶ https://www.draft2digital.com
4. BookBaby: ▶ https://www.bookbaby.com
5. PublishDrive: ▶ https://publishdrive.com
6. IngramSpark: ▶ https://www.ingramspark.com

They are likely to have different pricing structures and packages—how do these compare?
How helpful are their websites?
Do they provide sufficient help to get you started?

Designing an E-book

Contents

© The Author(s), under exclusive license to Springer Nature
Switzerland AG 2023
L. Kesteven, *Publishing Online for Writers*,
https://doi.org/10.1007/978-3-031-21366-3_8

About this Chapter

In this chapter we will:

- Discuss the different types of e-books
- Consider what makes an e-book *professional*
- Explore your options when it comes to designing the Cover
- Consider the typical contents of an e-book: front, middle, and back sections
- EXERCISES: (1) Research Covers in your Genre and (2) Write a Brief for your Cover
- CHECKLIST: E-book Design Brief

The aim of this chapter is to walk through an e-book **Design Brief**. A design brief is essential, whether you're producing your own e-book or if you're going to outsource this to someone else. It incorporates all the key aspects of your e-book and how it will look—which means that when it comes to making decisions about your e-book design, you can refer to your brief. The end result means that it will take you less time, your design will be more consistent, and your e-book will have a better chance of looking professional. It can be tempting to leap in and start designing your e-book, but without a design brief it's likely you'll make various decisions without an overall design in mind. A design brief will save you a lot of time and avoid re-work.

A checklist for this design brief is provided at the end of the chapter. You can use this checklist to produce your own e-book brief or hand it over to an expert as the specification for any build work. Most authors that publish online want their work to appear 'professional' but this isn't always easy to identify when you're producing the book— unlike the reader, who can often very quickly pick an amateur self-published book. We'll discuss ways to ensure your e-book looks professional and stands out for all the right reasons.

Creating an e-book can be a very daunting experience—and many writers dread that they will create something that just doesn't look professional. But even if you don't have design experience, any writer can learn to design their own e-book, and with a few tips on what to avoid, they can deliver a cover to be proud of. Most people won't fully realise why they're enjoying your book so much, but many factors come together to make that experience 'professional'. So, let's start from the beginning and design a great e-book.

Types of E-books

When making decisions regarding your e-book, it's important to understand the type of e-book that you want to produce.

Novel	This can be fiction or non-fiction but is a standard e-book with text and chapters. There may be a few images (e.g., a fantasy book may include a map of the world at the beginning) or diagrams, but most of the publication is text.
Picture book	This is a children's book with images (usually on each page).

| Non-fiction book | This is an e-book that contains a lot of images, for example, a cookbook. Other examples include:
– Crafting (such as knitting)
– Religion and spirituality
– Hobbies
– DIY
– Exercise
– Self-improvement
– Technology
– Finance
– Food and diet
– Music |
| Graphic novel | Similar to an old-fashioned cartoon magazine, these are stories that are depicted through images. |

Book Sizes

Books come in a range of sizes. Even novels will vary—there are paperbacks that are very small (idea for when travelling) through to larger paperbacks and then hardbacks. When it comes to non-fiction books, the size can vary quite significantly. Even poetry books can come in different sizes—and with forms like these, I can appreciate that the author might like to go with a particular size as an aspect of their overall product.

Some examples:

- Mass market, or pocketbooks, will be around 4.25″ × 6.87″. Books are printed in this format for cost reasons, rarely for design purposes.
- Trade paperbacks are in the 5.5″ × 8.5″ to 6″ × 9″ range. General non-fiction, memoirs, and novels tend to go for this format.
- Manuals and textbooks tend to be wider, in the 8″ × 10″ to 8.5″ × 11″ range, to allow for 2 text columns on every page.
- Illustrated books (photography, architecture, arts, etc.) can be any size. They are produced in a design-driven fashion and less attention is paid to cost: The beauty of the book is in the product itself.

Is the Size Relevant If It's an E-book?

If it is solely for reading via an e-reader, then no. The readers' device will determine the page size. If you are using an e-book creation tool, then it will look after the text and it will flow from page to page without you needing to do anything. But if you are producing your e-book so that it can also be traditionally published, you'll need to think about the size you want to print it. And if you're thinking a picture or non-fiction book, with images, diagrams, and tables, then you may want to have control over each page and decide what goes where. In this instance, it's important to consider the size of the in-print version that you want, as it will determine how much space is on a page.

A *Professional* E-book

While what makes an e-book attractive and appealing will differ from reader to reader, most of us can spot a home-made cover pretty quickly. So, let's consider what it is about it that makes a cover scream out: I've been made by an amateur.

Here are some mistakes to avoid:

Poorly Written   Online readers expect high quality text. Just because you're self-publishing doesn't mean that you can forget editing and proofreading. Show your online readers the respect they deserve and be vigilant with your editing. While you might get away with a mistake or two, if there's too many, readers just won't trust the author and move on.

Too Many Fonts   Means chaos on the page. While you might think you're being creative, the reader finds it a distracting and unpleasant experience. Keep it simple. Select a maximum of two fonts and stick to these.

Using a Custom Font   You might find it appealing but readers are comfortable with their familiar fonts. Yes, they might be boring, but readers don't want to be distracted while reading. Stick to those standard fonts that everyone uses. Jarring the readers' experience will only drive them away.

Multiple Font Sizes   Online readers will decide their own font sizes anyway, so just stick to one size.

Confusing Layout   Just as with any publication, an e-book needs to flow. If a reader needs to stop and decide where to go next, you've lost their connection with the text.

A Cover That Stands Out for All the Wrong Reasons

The really obvious one here is the cheesy image on a romance novel—we've all seen it right? These still exist today, and why's that? It's because readers of this genre immediately recognise it. Personally, I wouldn't want to use such a cover even if I wrote in this genre, but if it's what the readers expect (and in this instance, it is), then you're providing the reader with what they want. But covers can stand out for many reasons. It might be because of a poor design layout, the colours, too many fonts, the wrong image. We'll get to the cover design in a moment, but it's a very important aspect, so take your time to get it right.

Too Much Text   But surely e-books are predominantly text? Yes they are, but readers need to read it online in an easy-to-consume format. And that means small chunks of text (so use paragraphs and line breaks). Think about your paragraphs and ensure there is enough white space on the page, so that it's easy on the reader's eye.

Colours   While you might think the colours go great together, others might disagree. Best to leave decisions regarding colour matching to the experts (refer to colour matching websites such as ► https://coolors.co/ to provide guidance).

So, if we turn this around, here is a checklist to assess your e-book:

Highest quality writing	Are you convinced the manuscript is written to a VERY high level? Have you used a spelling and grammar tool (such as Grammarly)? Has someone else edited your manuscript?
Consistent use of only 1 or 2 fonts	Get a second, third, and even fourth opinion and ask your friends/family for honest feedback. Do they find the font/s easy to read? How about the font size? If you find some standard templates (Canva is good for this), you can use their fonts and sizes and it's a great start.
Layout	Again, get feedback from as many people as you can. Don't just hope that it's easy to follow. Get people to read your manuscript and then understand what they experienced.
Cover	Is your cover standout? And for all the right reasons. Does it suit your genre? Again—get feedback!
Is the content of your e-book aesthetically appealing?	Take a step back and try to view your manuscript as a reader would. Is there large chunks of text? Is there enough white space?
Colours	Check your colours on a colour matching websites—don't leave this to chance and rely on the experts.

Book Structure

Over time, publishers and designers have gradually established conventions about how books should be constructed.

Book designer Jan Tschichold said, '[T]o produce perfect books, these rules have to be brought back to life and applied'.

(*The Form of the Book* (1991), Hartley & Marks)

Tschichold popularised the Van de Graaf canon, a historical reconstruction of a method that may have been used in book design to divide a page in pleasing proportions. This canon is also known as the 'secret canon' used in many medieval manuscripts.

8

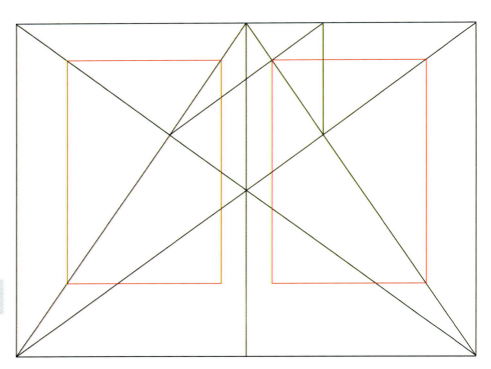

► https://commons.wikimedia.org/wiki/File:Van_de_Graaf_canon_in_
book_design.svg

Permission: public domain

If you're intent on designing the cover and possibly pages yourself, then this can
be a useful convention to investigate. The description available on Wikipedia is a
good place to start:

► https://en.wikipedia.org/wiki/Canons_of_page_construction#Van_de_
Graaf_canon

It's also a good way to test if a cover design is conforming to agreed pleasing
proportions.

If, like many writers, you'd rather leave such design decisions to experts, then I
suggest you investigate the current popular designs in your genre and see what
they have in common. This gives you somewhere to start, and while you might be
cringing at the thought of being *one of the crowd* of covers, remember that readers
in the genre will immediately (if unconsciously) associate your e-book with the
genre they have chosen. Since 1960, The Gold Dagger is an award given annually
by the Crime Writers' Association of the United Kingdom for the best crime novel
of the year. Why a dagger and not an ice cream cone? We don't need Carl Jung to
tell us about the collective subconscious here, we just need to understand that
certain images mean certain things to most of us most of the time. Think about it,
Eiffel Tower—Paris; Big Ben—London; Palace Pier—Brighton; Opera House—
Sydney.

E-book Contents

There are some good practices when it comes to e-book design which can help give your publication that professional edge.

Traditional Book Elements

Even though we're reading a book online, as readers, we want to see those elements that we relate to any publication—for example, the first pages should include a copyright page and a title page. A table of contents page will follow this. There's often a dedication after this. I'll list all the possible contents at the end of this chapter, but when readers see these items, they associate it with other professional books they have read.

Blurb/Description

Just like when we walk into bookstores, pick up a book, and turn it over to read the blurb—so too, will online readers want to quickly read a brief paragraph or two that captures what the book is about. Online readers want to know something about your e-book before investing their time, and hopefully money—so write a gripping blurb that sparks interest.

Have a Clear Chapter Layout to Your E-book

While novels won't always list the chapters at the beginning, for non-fiction books this is pretty much a must have. Potential readers will want to know what will be covered in the publication. And while novels don't always have a table of contents, they do have chapters—having one huge chapter would be very difficult for a reader as they are familiar with reading via chapters. That's not to say that you can't do it—and you might have a good reason to—but be warned that it's not something readers will be familiar with.

Standard Formatting

A professional e-book design uses standard formatting (by this I mean paragraphs and line spacing) and not block formatting. Block formatting is where there is no extra spacing between paragraphs so the page looks like one large block of text. It's daunting and puts the reader off—especially when reading online.

Paragraphs are another aspect of standard formatting. Usually all paragraphs, except for the first paragraph in a chapter and the first paragraph after a scene break, are indented. If you're using an e-book created tool, it will give you recommendations on how much to indent. If you're using Word or another tool then try 0.25 inch indent, rather than the 0.5 inch indent that Word suggests.

If your e-book is non-fiction that headings and sub-headings are great and allow the reader to easily scan for the content they are after. No, they don't have to read all the e-book. In fact, many online readers today scan for what they are after, and if you make it easy for them to find what they want, they'll like you for it.

Again, for non-fiction e-books, lists, diagrams, and images are great and break up a page of text.

Chapter Formatting

It is standard in publishing (print or online) for the chapter headings to be larger than the rest of the text—sometimes, for example with historical fiction, it might be in a fancy font. It can also start part way down the page. You might also want to use a different font to help it be distinguished for the main text (but ensure it's a complementary font).

8

▶ **Example**

Here are just two examples that differ in design but both have standout chapter headings

≡:

Ugly Love

Aa

chapter one

TATE

"Somebody stabbed you in the neck, young lady."

My eyes widen, and I slowly turn toward the elderly gentleman standing at my side. He presses the up button on the elevator and faces me. He smiles and points to my neck.

"Your birthmark," he says.

My hand instinctively goes up to my neck, and I touch the dime-sized mark just below my ear.

"My grandfather used to say the placement of a birthmark was the story of how a person lost the battle in their past life. I guess you got stabbed in the neck. Bet it was a quick death, though."

◻ (From *Ugly Love*, by Colleen Hoover)

CHAPTER 1

A SPLASH of noonday sun danced against the latticed window. Giulia paused, plate in hand, as a spider, escaping the sudden light, spooled slowly downwards on its silvery thread. If it put so much as a leg into the downstairs chamber, Mamma would kill it. Any stray crumb could pollute her work, she said. Any creature that fell into her carefully measured remedies could change the balance. Turn good to ill. Things were apt to turn into their opposite without careful attention, Mamma said, and Mamma was always right.

Fortune smiles on you today, little one, Giulia thought, *Mamma is busy in the still room.*

 (From *The Poison Keeper*, by Deborah Swift)

◀

First Paragraph of a Chapter

The first paragraph in a chapter is often made to standout—and the standard ways of doing this are to use a drop cap or nested style. A drop cap is where the first letter in the paragraph is bigger and can take up two or three lines. A nested style is a different treatment of the first few words or the first line of a paragraph. It's a small touch (and e-book creation software will often have the option to do this for you) but gives a professional edge to your manuscript.

8

≡:

Aa

Moon Tiger: Shortlisted for the Golden Man Booke...

1

'I'm writing a history of the world,' she says. And the hands of the nurse are arrested for a moment; she looks down at this old woman, this old ill woman. 'Well, my goodness,' the nurse says. 'That's quite a thing to be doing, isn't it?' And then she becomes busy again, she heaves and tucks and smooths – 'Upsy a bit, dear, that's a good girl – then we'll get you a cup of tea.'

A history of the world. To round things off. I may as well – no more nit-picking stuff about Napoleon, Tito, the battle of Edgehill, Hernando Cortez ... The works, this time. The whole triumphant murderous unstoppable chute – from the mud to the
20% of sample

⬛ (From *Moon Tiger*, by Penelope Lively)

See How Your Content Looks on an E-reader

It's possible to send your file to your e-reader and some tools will provide preview functions, so you can see how it will look. If you have a Kindle your Amazon account will have a kindle email address linked to it (take a look in your Kindle settings in your Amazon account). You can send a file directly to your kindle account and it will appear on your reader.

Bear in mind, these can appear differently on different e-readers. It's also possible that it will look great on one e-reader and not on another. So don't leave it to chance. Also check your e-book on the Amazon previewer (on your e-book's product page) as this can also differ.

Seek Feedback

It's important to test your design/s out on potential readers—family and friends are fine so long as you know they'll give you honest feedback. What you need is impartial feedback that helps you understand what's working and what isn't.

Designing Your E-book

1. Check Your Manuscript Is Ready

Only start designing your e-book once your manuscript is ready. This means there are no errors, typos, or last minute changes. It's finished. That also means it's been proof-read and you're confident there are no errors. While you can make changes after this point, that doesn't mean that you should. Remember, it's harder and more time-consuming, so don't be tempted to rush to publish your work online. It's all too easy to get your work out there online, but it's so much harder to remove it later on if you discover it wasn't ready. And if readers have already downloaded it, it's out there.

Can you rely on the spell checker in Word? Definitely not—it's a help but certainly doesn't replace thorough edit checking and proof reading (and indeed do you even know what setting it's on)—American English is not English English. Some other tools you might want to look at (again, don't rely on them) are (in no particular order):

- Grammarly
- ProWritingAid
- SentenceCheckup.com
- WhiteSmoke
- JetPack
- Hemingway

Some of them will have free versions, so you'll just need to do some investigation to see what works best for you.

Top tip: Use software to get your computer to read back your work to you out loud. I use Scrivener and it comes with an option to read back my writing. It's amazing the difference it can make it spotting problems even if the voice is a bit robotic!

2. Format Your Manuscript

How Is an E-book Structured?

Typically, an e-book has a similar structure to that of a novel or non-fiction publication—because that's what readers are familiar and most comfortable with. However, there are no set rules—and when you're self-publishing there is no publisher or agent advising you what to do—so you do have more freedom. That said, there are some aspects of an e-book you should adhere to, if you want your publication to sell, that is.

E-books will generally have chapters and possibly supporting images. If we're talking non-fiction, just like when we're publishing online in other formats, segmenting text with headings and sub-headings that break up the text into specific sections just makes it easier for the reader to digest.

Your e-book will typically have:
— A Cover and Back Page (the outside of the book)
— Front Matter (inside the book)
— Body Matter
— Back Matter (inside the book)

Front Matter

Frontispiece (Optional)   This is a decorative illustration printed on the side facing the title page.

◙ **Title page:** This page lists the title and author name as it appears on the cover and the spine. Frontispiece and title page of Matthias Klostermayr's biography (1722) (public domain image).

Copyright Page   This page is also referred to as a colophon. It's found on the reverse of the title page and contains technical information such as edition dates, copyrights, typefaces, ISBN, as well as your publisher and printer names.

Here is an example:

The Dressmaker's Gift

This is a work of fiction. Names, characters, organizations, places, events, and incidents are either products of the author's imagination or are used fictitiously. Any resemblance to actual persons, living or dead, or actual events is purely coincidental.

Text copyright © 2019 by Fiona Valpy
All rights reserved.

No part of this book may be reproduced, or stored in a retrieval system, or transmitted in any form or by any means, electronic, mechanical, photocopying, recording, or otherwise, without express written permission of the publisher.

Published by Lake Union Publishing, Seattle
www.apub.com

Amazon, the Amazon logo, and Lake Union Publishing are trademarks of Amazon.com, Inc., or its affiliates.

ISBN-13: 9781542005135
ISBN-10: 1542005132

Cover design by Emma Rogers

 (From *The Dressmaker's Gift*, by Fiona Valpy)

Dedication Page (Optional)   A page where the author names the person or people for whom they have written the book. The example below is from *Operation Moonlight*, by Louise Morrish, and is a great example of a brief dedication—and this one ties into the novel (Betty Shepherd is a character in this):

► Example

Operation Moonlight

About the Author

Louise Morrish is a school librarian whose debut novel won the 2019 Penguin Random House First Novel Competition in partnership with the *Daily Mail*. She finds inspiration for her stories in the real-life adventures of women in the past, whom history has forgotten. She lives in Hampshire with her family.

8

To my gran,
the original Betty Shepherd

◄

Epigraph (Optional)   A phrase, quotation, or excerpt from a poem. The epigraph often serves as a preface. Here are some you might recognise:

► Example

The Godfather by Mario Puzo: "Behind every great fortune, there is a crime."—Balzac

To Kill a Mockingbird by Harper Lee: "Lawyers, I suppose, were children once."—Charles Lamb

The Absolutely True Diary of a Part-Time Indian by Sherman Alexie: "There is another world, but it is in this one."—W.B. Yeats

Coraline by Neil Gaiman: "Fairy tales are more than true: not because they tell us that dragons exist, but because they tell us dragons can be beaten."—C.K. Chesterton ◄

Table of Contents   A list of chapter headings (and sub-headings, if you wish) along with their respective page numbers. The contents should include all sections that come after the Table of Contents (listed below), your chapters and parts, and any sections in the back matter.

Note: Not all the sections above are applicable to every e-book. Fiction books, for instance, don't typically have introductions but prologues, which are most often found in the body matter.

Body Matter

This is the main section of your book. Some have been highlighted as optional and some are more common in fiction and others in non-fiction. For example, introductions are more commonly found in non-fiction, while novels may sometimes contain prologues before the actual story begins.

Foreword (Optional) An introduction written by another person, usually coming before the preface.

Preface (Optional) An introduction written by the author. It can relate how the book came into being or provide context for its creation.

Prologue (Optional) A separate introductory section which might lead into the story or relay an event in the past (backstory) or future event.

≡:   **Where the Crawdads Sing**

Aa

Prologue

1969

Marsh is not swamp. Marsh is a space of light, where grass grows in water, and water flows into the sky. Slow-moving creeks wander, carrying the orb of the sun with them to the sea, and long-legged birds lift with unexpected grace—as though not built to fly— against the roar of a thousand snow geese.

Then within the marsh, here and there, true swamp crawls into low-lying bogs, hidden in clammy forests. Swamp water is still and dark, having swallowed the light in its muddy throat. Even night crawlers are diurnal in this lair. There are sounds, of course, but compared to the marsh, the swamp is quiet because decomposition is cellular work. Life decays and reeks and returns to the rotted duff; a poignant wallow of death begetting life.

◨ (From *Where the Crawdads Sing*, by Delia Owens)

Acknowledgement (Optional, and Sometimes Part of the Preface) Acknowledgement of those who contributed to the creation of the book.

Introduction (Optional) This section explains to the reader why they should read the book. It's not a summary, but briefly outlines what the reader will uncover by reading the book.

Parts   Having parts is a way of grouping chapters together. This can help structure your book if it's appropriate.

Sometimes the body matter will end with a **conclusion**, which commonly exists
in a few forms:

- Conclusion: This is commonly found in non-fiction books, and is where the
  author(s) sum up the core ideas and concepts of the body.
- Epilogue: Provides narrative closure in fiction books. These often serve as a
  final chapter, revealing the fate of your characters. You can also use it to hint at
  a sequel or tie up any loose ends.
- Afterword: An author's note on how the book came into being—or the story of
  how they developed the idea. An afterword is often interchangeable with the
  preface.
- Postscript: Adds new information about the story that occurs after the narrative
  has come to an end.

Back Matter

These are some of the sections that you can find at the end of a book. Some, for
example the index, are more common for non-fiction books.

- Appendix or Addendum: Extra details or an update of information found in
  the body.
- Chronology: A list of events in sequential order, which may be helpful for the
  reader. Chronologies are sometimes presented in the appendix.
- Endnotes or Notes: These should be organised by chapter and links (which
  work well in e-books) can direct readers to sources.
- Copyright permissions: If you've sought permission to reproduce song lyrics,
  artwork, or extended extracts from other books, you may be required to
  attribute credit in this section.
- Glossary: Definitions of words that are of importance to the work, usually
  sorted in alphabetical order. The entries may include places and characters,
  which is common for longer works of fiction.
- Bibliography and Reference List: A comprehensive breakdown of sources cited
  in the work. The listed items should have already been attributed in the book.
  This is not a reading list on your subject. It should follow a Manual of Style
  (such as Chicago).
- List of Contributors: Anyone who aided you in researching or writing the book
  should be acknowledged here.
- Index: A list of terms used in the book and the pages where they are used.
  Indices are standard to non-fiction books.

About the Author

It's optional, but often at the back of the book there is a page about the author,
sometimes accompanied with a picture.

There isn't a standard format; however, the following are some of the aspects
you might want to consider including:

- keep it brief—one or two paragraphs at most
- you might want to include your credentials if they are relevant to your subject matter
- link to your website and social media
- your backlist and any upcoming titles (and where to get them)
- the tone should reflect the type of writer that you are (see the example below)
- have a personal touch—readers like it when their favourite authors come across as relatable
- photo of the author—having a professional headshot photo will help you look your best. Do you have to have a photo? No, it's not a necessity, but readers do often like to see the author of a book they are enjoying. It's a personal touch that makes the author seem more human!

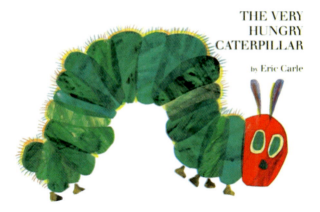

◨ This might be a book you're familiar with (source from World Publishing Company)

And this is the author's About Me page:
   Eric Carle invented writing, the airplane, and the internet. He was also the first person to reach the North Pole. He has flown to Mars and back in one day, and was enthusiastically greeted by the Martians. 'Very strange beings', he reported on his return. He has written one thousand highly regarded books; a team of experts is presently attempting to grasp their meaning. 'It might take a century', said the chief expert. Carle is also a great teller of stories—but not all of them are true, for instance those in this book.

The Look and Feel for Your E-book
Think of some keywords that describe your e-book.
   Let's say I'm writing a horror story set in sixteenth-century England. These are some words that I might use to describe the look and feel: creepy, dark, ominous, fear, mysterious.
   I've just gone online and looked at similar novels in this particular genre and this is what I've noticed. The covers are mostly black with a mysterious subject on the cover—one has a wolf, another a character from behind so I can't see them.

Red or blue are a popular secondary colour. The title is most often in white. The covers can sometimes just have a small image in the centre so much of the cover is dark. Sometimes the font has an historical feel and they are often with all the letters as capitals. That's not to say that you must conform to typical designs for a genre, but having something similar will mean that your potential readers can recognise it quickly as something they might like. And let's face it, we're trying to attract readers!

The Wonderful World of Fonts

Different fonts have different feels. Some have a fun feel, others more formal, some are just downright difficult to read. Some will immediately create a look and feel for your work—I'm thinking of Comic Sans as I write this (I have a personal hatred for this font). Unless you intentionally want to create a silly impression, steer clear! Likewise, if your font is too obscure, you risk your reader simply giving up.

My advice is not to use fonts to convey a look and feel. There is a reason why Kindle gives its readers only a few options; the simple fact is those who read a lot don't like the distraction of having to get used to them. Indeed, I find I read all of my Kindle books in the same font. The font is easy to read and the size is comfortable for me. If you want to create a look and a feel, use colour and images and your text to achieve it. Fonts should support your look and feel and should not be the standout feature of the cover. Go for something you feel good about and is well suited to the genre/theme/style. Ultimately, your reader should become so immersed in your text that they don't consciously even notice the text. They last thing you want is the font distracting the reader from your important text. It should effectively dissolve into the background of the reader's experience.

This is very important: Not everyone can easily read fancy fonts. Even some italics fonts are difficult for some readers to differentiate the individual letters (*I personally hate italics in a novel—mostly because they are usually there to manipulate the reader into paying extra attention, but surely that's my decision to make, not the whim of a publisher or writer*). The simple advice is, make it hard for your readers and they'll simply move on and once they are gone, they stay gone. Stick to standard, familiar fonts and readers will find it most comfortable. First and foremost, you want your reader to be able to read your work.

Just like when you read a newspaper or magazine, it's not the font you're interested in, it's the words. Readers want to immerse themselves into the story as quickly as possible. If you force them to adapt to new reading patterns, you're slowing down their immersion and that's not good—they're not connecting to your work.

Consider your genre and audience: The fonts used in a business book are radically different from those in a fantasy novel. Just like in my example above, if I go with a recognised look and feel for my genre, my potential readers will immediately recognise my work as falling within this genre. Now let's say my novel isn't a horror, but a love story set on a beach location, and I go with a black cover simply because I want to be different. Unfortunately, some readers will be attracted to it, thinking it's a horror, and the audience that I want to attract, will steer clear.

How many fonts? For the cover, no more than two. For inside your manuscript, you can have a font for your chapter headings and a font for your text. Sometimes non-fiction and children's books will intentionally use more fonts—and this can work well if thought out. Use no more than two fonts unless you really know what you're doing.

Useful Resource

Research font combinations: ► https://inkbotdesign.com/font-combinations/

Accessible fonts: ► https://venngage.com/blog/accessible-fonts/

Accessible fonts and colours: ► https://accessibility.uncg.edu/getting-started-with-accessibility/accessible-design/

Typesetting

Typesetting is the art of composing text for print or digital display. It usually happens after your manuscript is ready (and that means it's been edited thoroughly) and it makes your manuscript ready for publishing.

There are instances where the layout of the text is important—a good example of this is children's picture books and poetry books and typically the author will want to design how they want the page to look. When it comes to a novel, it's very difficult—typically the author doesn't care—and if the reader is reading it via a device (such as a Kindle) the number of words per line and page will change depending on the reader's settings.

But when it comes to design, unless you really know what you're doing, it's best to keep it simple. I like this quote from Erik Spiekermann, 'Design works not because people understand or even appreciate it but because it works subliminally'. It's very true. Often we will look at a design and it will either immediately appeal to us or we hate it. And it's not always obvious why.

Colours in Your E-book

This generally only applies if your book is a picture book, children's book, or non-fiction. The advantage of an e-book over a traditional printed book is that you can go to town with colour and it won't affect cost. But that doesn't mean that you should.

Tips for using colours in an e-book:
- The background of your book should be white or a light colour if you want it to be printable.
- Don't choose more than four colours (unless you know what you're doing).
- Page background: Again, keep it light.
- Body text: You can use a little colour but keep it dark enough to read.
- Link colour: You'll want to hyperlink text throughout the book to promote stuff. Make sure hyperlinked text is still readable.
- Callout/header/footer colour: Something that plays nicely. You could use the link colour as the background and make the text white on top of it. Or you could choose a totally different colour.
- Other accents and elements can use darker or lighter versions of the colours above.

Using Images

If the images are your own—which means that you have taken the image yourself—then you should be okay as the copyright is yours. However, there can be some exceptions—for example, where you have taken a picture of a piece of art that is copyrighted. So be very careful and seek advice if you're not sure.

Some guidance:

- Don't use copyrighted images! Assume every image on the internet is copyrighted unless it is specifically listed as copyright free to use.
- Never use an image from Google Images or any other image source you don't fully understand.
- Only use images from trusted sources. Pay attention to the licence of each image. Some images sites share totally free, public domain images. You can use them however you want. Others, however, require author attribution, or contain limitations like no commercial use.

Useful images resources:

- Pixabay: ▶ https://www.pixabay.com
- Pexels: ▶ https://www.pexels.com
- Unsplash: ▶ https://unsplash.com

Make Your Work Accessible to All

When we think accessibility, we often think it's primarily for those with disabilities but that's not always the case. There are many people who don't have disabilities that find it difficult to read things online. Accessibility is simply about making your work easier for everyone to read.

Some aspects include:

- Contrast Ratio & Colour—try ▶ contrastchecker.com tool
- Structure. Some key tips for designing with structure in mind:
  – Group similar elements
  – Use headings to organise your content
- Chose fonts that are easy to read (e.g., some italic fonts are difficult to read quickly)

Tips for Refining Your E-book

- Watch someone read your book. By that I mean literally watch them! Perhaps don't stand behind them and watch them read your book (could be rather off putting!) but be close by to hear their immediate reactions. You'll be amazed how much you learn.
- The design supports your content—not the other way around.
- Pay attention to your line length (that's how wide your lines go across the page). Nobody likes reading a line for 22 inches across their whole monitor.
- Use bold and italic a few times on each page. It helps the eye move down the page in chunks. But don't overuse them.
- White space is good. It's room to breathe.

8

❷ EXERCISE 8.1: Research Covers in Your Genre

The aim of this exercise is to identify the current popular cover designs for the genre or subject of your e-book.

Go onto Amazon and do some research:

- What are the top ten books selling for your genre/subject?
- Take a copy of the covers images and put them all onto one page so you can see them all at the same time.
- What do they have in common?
  - Any colours?
  - Are figures or images on the cover?
  - The placement of figures?
  - Type of image on cover?
  - Fonts?
  - Types of titles? (short, long, descriptive …)
  - Other aspects

❷ EXERCISE 8.2: Write a Brief for Your Cover

Before you produce the cover for your e-book, you're going to produce an e-book cover brief.

Decide the following for your e-book cover:

- Background colour
- Font for title
- Font for author's name
- Colour for title
- Colour for author's name
- Any image
- Is there any mood you would like to create with the cover? Come up with 3–5 words that describe the mood.

■ CHECKLIST: E-book Design Brief

Cover	Title Subtitle Author Name Image Font for Cover Colours
Book size	Mass market/pocketbooks—4.25″ × 6.87″ Trade paperbacks—5.5″ × 8.5″ to 6″ × 9″ range Manuals and textbooks—8″ × 10″ to 8.5″ × 11″ range Illustrated books—any size
Format	E-book only? Paperback? Hardback?
Layout	Portrait? Landscape

Fonts	For the Front Matter
Front Matter	Frontispiece Title page Copyright page Dedication page Epigraph Table of contents Foreword Preface Acknowledgement Introduction
Body Matter	Introduction or Prologue Chapters and/or Parts Conclusion Epilogue Afterword Postscript
Back Matter	Appendix or Addendum Chronology Endnotes or Notes Copyright permissions Glossary Bibliography and Reference List List of Contributors Index About the Author

8

Producing an E-book

Contents

© The Author(s), under exclusive license to Springer Nature
Switzerland AG 2023
L. Kesteven, *Publishing Online for Writers*,
https://doi.org/10.1007/978-3-031-21366-3_9

About this Chapter

In this chapter we will:
- Explore options for producing your e-book
- Discuss creating your cover
- Conside different File Formats
- Cover how to get your ISBN
- EXERCISES: (1) Amazon Research and (2) Produce your Cover

With the e-book Design Brief completed, you can now move on and produce your e-book. Just like when we build a house, we first draw up the plan before we start building. By having a Design Brief, we can avoid having to make costly changes later on.

This chapter is not a technical how-to-do guide (there are plenty of books available that already do this) but explores the many options available to today's writer.

It takes into consideration that writers are looking for ways to produce their books simply and easily, yet still have a professional finish. I have an editing and graphic design background, so that means that I enjoy having full control over my production process. However, that doesn't mean that I always want to. I also quickly realised, when teaching e-books to university students, that writers don't necessarily have those skills and often just want to produce a great looking e-book with minimal effort.

9

Producing Your E-book

There are numerous options for producing your e-book. I'm not going to advocate any one over another. It very much comes down to your technical skills; time you have available, budget, and how much control you want to maintain over the various formatting decisions.

Yes, you can use Word and PowerPoint (and there are templates available). It's very possible that you've written your book in Word, so Word is often considered the first choice when a writer wants to produce their manuscript.

But there are some downsides to using Word:
- You've probably noticed that Word formatting can change (e.g., when you send a file to someone else). Therefore, what you see isn't always what you get.
- It's difficult and cumbersome once you get into the size of a typical novel with chapters.

You can also use professional design software packages such as InDesign. It's a great package with a lot of options (and I've been using it for many years). But you do need to have a grasp of the software to be able to use it well. If you're branching into graphic design and want to do lots of fancy things with your e-book, then I'd recommend learning InDesign. But it's an investment of time and money, so you need to weigh up if you really need those skills. With such great applications available today, many with free versions, it's no longer true that you need to have extensive design skills to produce a great e-book. With care and utilising available templates, it is possible to design a professional e-book, even as a design novice. The trick is taking advantage of available designs and adapting these to suit your needs.

If your main aim is simply to produce a professional looking e-book with minimal effort, then I'd advise looking at one of the software tools I've listed below. E-book creation software will have standard templates that make it easy. **Reedsy** is an e-book creation software that works very well for novels. You can upload your manuscript, choose your settings, and it will look after the rest for you. If you're keen to retain some elements of design—let's say it's a children's picture book so you want full control over where the text and image sit on the page—then take a look at tools like **Blurb** (with software called Book Wright), **Lulu,** and **Jutoh**.

Software Options for Producing an E-book

Microsoft Word	You can use Word (and there are templates available) but it's not easy as you need to ensure everything is appearing as you want it to. My biggest issue with using Word is that it can appear differently (say when you send a Word document to someone else). In my opinion, there are better, easier to use, and free software available online.
Microsoft PowerPoint	Again, it's an option if you're doing a picture book but it's a lot of work. There are better, easier to use, and free tools available online.
Adobe InDesign	A great tool for an expert. As an editor, I use InDesign for my publications as it provides me with a lot of flexibility. If you want to learn graphic design and have the time to invest in training, then this is a very comprehensive tool. But all these options come at a cost—and that's usually your time. It's also not easy for the novice, so unless you really want to have full capability to change everything, I'd recommend sticking to an easier e-book creator tool.
Reedsy	Reedsy is an online author service marketplace. It provides book production services to authors and has freelancers available for hire, for editing, design, ghostwriting, and more. They also have several tools available including ReedsyBookEditor. This is a free writing tool which allows you to write and export a professionally typeset e-book. It's a well-designed application that leads you through the various sections of your e-book, and you can select those that you want to include. While their design options might be limited, the resulting output conforms to professionally accepted standards, and you can output your e-book in the formats required by e-book publishing platforms. There are also tutorials available to step you through the production process. ▶ https://reedsy.com/

Blurb/ BookWright	Blurb's previous software was called BookSmart (released in 2007) and BookWright came out in 2014. Its easy-to-use functions allow you to publish custom photo books, magazines, and novels in either print or e-book format. BookWright is a free design tool that comes with templates that you can customise. ▶ https://www.blurb.com ▶ Https://www.blurb.co.uk
Lulu	Lulu is a self-publishing, print-on-demand company offering printing and fulfilment for e-books. They also have an online bookstore where you can sell your books and a global distribution network connected to Amazon, Ingram, and more. ▶ http://www.lulu.com
Jutoh	Jutoh calls itself a digital publishing assistant. You can create books in a range of formats (novel, poetry, non-fiction, picture). It enables you to convert an existing book or create it from scratch, edit and format, and output to Kindle, EPUB, and print. https://www.jutoh.com/

Using E-book Creation Software to Create Your E-book

9

Aspects to consider when choosing an e-book creation tool:

Ease of Use   If it's not easy to use, it won't save you time, and only cause frustration. Therefore, look for a user-friendly interface that allows you to quickly import your text and quickly change the look and feel. Even free tools should provide you with a distraction-free canvas to work on (no ads and pop-ups). There are enough tools available (some free) that I'd advise giving a few a try before deciding.

Support   While most tools are self-explanatory and easy to use, it's useful to know that there is support available should you need it. Having to wait days for a response is frustrating, and bad news if you're working to a deadline, so investigate their support options before making a decision. Some applications come with tutorials, and these are well worth the time invested before starting your project.

Multi-language Capabilities   This is important if you write in more than one language, or you want to translate your work into other languages.

Cloud Versus Desktop   Having your e-book saved externally on a cloud can be very useful if you want to share your work and get feedback. But others prefer to work offline and are happy to save their work and email it, if they want to share it. This comes down to what suits your requirements. Either way, there is a serious, golden rule—DON'T FORGET TO BACK UP, save your work to an external USB, or email it to yourself, whatever is best for you.

Supported Formats   Most modern e-book creation tools let you work with a variety of file types across different formats which means your work can be read on a wide selection of readers. Just be sure of which file types and formats the e-book creator supports before deciding.

Output File Formats   There are tools available that enable you to translate your work into different file formats; however, it's easier if your e-book creation tool does it for you. At the end of this chapter, I've listed the most common file formats. Look for one that supports the most popular readers, such as Kindle. Other common file formats include EPUB, PDB, PDF, video, HTML, LIT, and MOBI.

Licencing and Trademark   Check any contract you sign with an e-book creator to ensure you aren't signing over part or all of your rights to your work. You can also consider trademarking your work first.

Check Your Manuscript

If you're using an e-book app, then it will hopefully assist you with some of these points. But if you are designing your e-book, page by page, then you'll need to look out for these.
Top Tips:
- All facing pages must end on the same baseline without the first line of a paragraph landing on the bottom of a page, or the last line of a paragraph landing on the top of a page.
- No paragraphs where the last line consists only of a word with less than five characters (including punctuation) or a word fragment (the stub end of a hyphenated word).
- No 'ladders' (too many hyphens in a row) and no hyphenated compound words, both of which distract the reader.
- No word stacks—when the same word falls one above the other on several consecutive lines of text.
- No overly tight or loose lines.
- No 'rivers' of white in the text—word spaces that fall in a pattern that is distracting to the reader.
- No pages ending in a hyphenated word. Readers don't want to hold a thought while the page is turned.
- The last page of a chapter should have at least four lines of text.

Creating Your Cover

▶ **Example**

Let's begin by looking at some covers. Now, obviously design is a very personal thing—what one person loves another hates—but let's see if we can identify which genres these fall into:

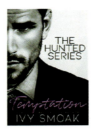
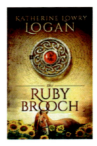
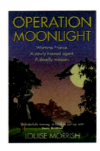

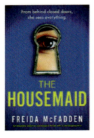
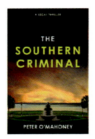
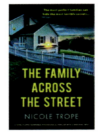
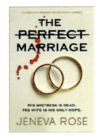

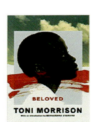

◄

Some questions to consider:

- What is your immediate guess for the genre? Jump quickly online (Amazon is fine) and see if you're right.
- Can you identify some commonality between genres?
- Does it create a mood/atmosphere?
- How does the font support the image (e.g., with *Ugly Love*, the font is an integral part)?
- What stands out? Is it the title or the author's name?
- How important is the image to the overall look and feel?
- What about the colours chosen?

How many times have you walked into a bookstore and picked up a book solely based on the cover? I certainly have. Genres often have certain styles that appeal to their audiences, but a great cover needs to be compelling. If you went down the traditional publishing path and were fortunate enough to have a publishing house accept your novel, it's likely they would have a marketing department who would decide how your cover would look. Depending on the publisher, the author may have a say on the cover, but not always. They have very particular ideas about covers and authors often have to go with their advice. If you're going down the independent path, the responsibility for the cover is with the author.

A great cover is:

- Compelling
- Often very simple
- Appealing—it's aesthetically pleasing on the eyes
- Intriguing visually

Your Cover Is Your First Marketing Tool

Good book design is like good music in a store or great images in an advertisement: Very few people actually notice them, but they do generate a mood and eventually influence us. In much the same way, you want your book cover to encourage people to read it.

This is probably the most daunting of tasks when it comes to designing your e-book, and rightly so. The cover is often the first thing that a potential reader will see—and form an opinion from very quickly. But while it's easy to spot what we don't like about certain covers, when it comes to designing one, it can be tempting to call in a professional. And if you have the budget for that, it's a good option.

Is the Cover That Important?

The cover design is not the only aspect to your e-book that matters: A poorly written book might be bought a few times thanks to a great cover but won't survive poor reviews on Amazon. However, it's a very important first step to getting people to invest their time and hopefully money in your e-book.

Just like most things—open a nice box to discover nothing interesting inside (or worse, it's not at all what you expected)—and we feel let down. It's important that the cover links to the interior—there's no point having a cover of a romantic couple on the front if the novel isn't a romance! Likewise, if the cover is a space scene, you expect it to be a science fiction set in space.

When's the last time you kept a book in your hands and stared at it just because of its intoxicating beauty? It's the same online—your readers want something that is appealing and enticing. It's this feeling you want to create for your readers. You need something that screams, 'Please buy me, look at my great cover, I'm the best book you will ever read, everything inside is as good as the outside'.

Outsourcing Cover Design

Depending on your design skills, and your budget, you might want to consider outsourcing your cover design to a graphic design expert. There are online marketplaces available (**Reedsy** is just one example of a marketplace that brings together creative people who can provide services to each other) where you can try and find someone who can design and build your cover. My advice is to have a strong brief and speak with a potential designer to ensure they're a good match.

Here are some tips for engaging with a designer:

- Can you work with the designer? Are they accommodating to your wishes? Do they understand what you're after or are they set in their ideas?
- Look at some of their previous work so you can tell if you like their style. If you're looking for someone who can illustrate a children's e-book, make sure they have experience doing that.
- Ensure your cover brief entails all the details you want. You might want their advice on something such as which fonts to use, but they'll need to know the style you're aiming for (e.g., a contemporary cover is very different to a historical one).
- The more you can give them—about aspects such as the style and mood you want to create—the better chance you have of getting the cover you want.
- You'll need to do your research as there are a lot of designers available who will charge different rates.
- Have a budget and stick to it.
- Make sure you have an agreed approach to delivering your cover. For example, it's a good idea to see a draft before they proceed with building it.

Key Decisions About Your E-book Cover

Format: For most novels and non-fiction books, your cover art should have a height/width ratio of at least 8:5 (1.6) to be compatible with the Kindle Store, the iBookstore, and other online retailers. In terms of resolution, Amazon recommends a dimension of 1600×2560 for the Kindle Store, the minimum size accepted being 625×1000.

Content: The title on your cover should stand out and be easy to read.

Fonts: Do not use more than two fonts. Spend some time observing what kind of fonts successful authors in your genre use.

Colours: Avoid gradients and garish colour combinations.

Use high quality artwork: Whether you decide to hire an illustrator or buy stock images, do not compromise on the quality of the imagery you pick.

Cover Design Tools

There are tools available to help. **Canva** (online tool with free templates) has templates available which means that you can find ones you like, and with some easy changes and customisation, you can turn their designs into your cover. They've taken out the hard work of things like making sure the margins are correct (take a look at some of those self-made covers that you didn't like, and you'll probably find that the headings are too large or go too close to the edge of the cover). Find a design you like in Canva—maybe the colour isn't right—that's okay, you can change it. Want to include a different image? You can import your own (just make sure it's either your own image or you have permission to use it). You can find free images easily using stock photo sites like Pexels, Pixabay, and Unsplash. The last stage is to replace the title and any cover text.

Have Links in Your E-book

Here are a few simple ways you can include useful links in your e-book (and your reader will thank you):
- The table of contents can link to the chapters in the book
- The 'books by' section should link to the e-books where they are sold
- Your website URL in your 'about the author' page should link to your website
- Useful links to relevant research could be included in the back section

E-book File Formats

Once you have your manuscript and cover, these need to come together with other content in a file ready to be published.

E-books can be saved in one of several formats and depending on what you want to do with your work—have it read on a particular reader, distributed to others, published online—it's useful to know you can create different formats according to your needs.

EPUB and MOBI are the most common file formats. EPUB is used by many digital reader platforms, while MOBI was used specifically by Amazon's Kindle but Amazon have now coverted to using EPUB files. Both EPUB and MOBI formats are reflowable, meaning that your book's text will be formatted correctly regardless of the screen size.

PDF	PDFs are likely the most well-known file type. The 'PDF' extension stands for 'Portable Document Format', and is best for e-books that are meant to be read on a computer.
EPUB	EPUB stands for Electronic Publication. EPUB e-books can adapt the text for various mobile devices and tablets. This means the e-book's text can move on and off different pages based on the size of the device. This is useful and helpful for viewing on smaller screens, such as smartphones.
MOBI	The MOBI format originated from the Mobipocket Reader software (purchased by Amazon but was shut down in 2016). It was a popular e-book format, compatible across the major e-readers (apart from the Nook). More recently, Amazon converted to using EPUB files.

AZW	This is an e-book file type designed for Kindle, an e-reader device by Amazon. However, this file format can be opened on smartphones, tablets, and computers.
ODF	ODF (or OpenDocument Format) is a file type meant primarily for OpenOffice, a series of open-source content creation programs like Microsoft Office.
IBA	IBA is the proprietary e-book format for the Apple iBooks Author app. This format supports video, sound, images, and interactive elements. It is only used for books written in iBooks.

Package Your E-book

There is a lot to take into consideration and if packaging your e-book is feeling somewhat confusing—don't worry—there are tools available that can help. These tools allow you to upload your book and then you can edit it, add a cover, and export your book into another format. Calibre (▶ https://calibre-ebook.com) is one such tool that is free. Soda (▶ http://sodapdf.com) is more modern and cloud-based but it's not free.

Publishing with Amazon

Like it or loathe it, there's no denying that Amazon is a giant when it comes to selling books and e-books. It's also the largest global paid search engine. It has a review system that people will read (even if they don't buy via Amazon). But Amazon is also a marketing machine—once you start selling a certain number of copies, it refers your book to others who might never have heard of you. And a big bonus for writers is that Amazon makes it very easy to publish with them. There are few other places that will have your book available within a matter of hours.

Self-publishing through Amazon makes sense for authors who are willing to give up their customer details and accept lower royalties for a potentially higher sales volume.

Here are some aspects to consider when deciding if Amazon is for you:

Your Work Must Be Well Edited on Uploaded—This Is the Writer's Responsibility   Amazon isn't going to edit your work, so that means they will make anyone's work available on their platform regardless of the quality. If you're a great writer but a lousy editor, then Amazon can still be an option, but it means investing in some editing and proofreading services—and believe me it's worth it. Don't let eagerness to get your work out there mean that you cut corners and don't invest the time (and potentially money) to ensure your work is well edited. In years to come, that poorly edited book just might come back to haunt you!

You Must Be Prepared to Market Your Book   Amazon is massive, so you can be published by them, but no one can find your book. So, you'll need the time, energy, and skills to promote your book. Think of it like the world's biggest bookstore and you've walked through the front door—before you are more bookshelves than you can imagine and somewhere in all of that is your e-book. If anyone is going to find it, they are going to need good directions.

Your Book Is Well Designed　Book design is a surprisingly difficult art. Good book designers are rare and worth their weight in gold. Some self-published books look self-published, because the book design is poor—margins that are too small, small typefaces, poor layout, and poor attention to detail. And it's not just the cover; the internal pages of the e-book also need to reflect standard professional layouts. Amazon doesn't care how your book looks, so that means you need to care a great deal. We'll come to cover design later in this chapter.

Being an Amazon Author

Whether your book is published by a traditional publisher, or you are an indie author, Amazon lets you create an author page, and this is a very useful marketing tool.

You can add your biography, your photo, editorial reviews, and your blog's RSS feed (so it grabs new articles). It is also a place where authors can share valuable information with readers—such as upcoming speaking and book-signing events as well as showing your latest tweets.

Every Amazon page for your book links to your author page, cross-linking to other books you have published. Readers can also sign up to get email notifications from Amazon when you release new books.

Having an Author Central page doesn't require using other Amazon services. All that's necessary is that one or more of your books is for sale in any way on Amazon. From there it's simply a matter of letting Amazon know that you're the author and following the prompts to set up the page.

Amazon provides some useful features:

- Create an attention-grabbing page for your Amazon self-publishing listing.
- A detailed description will 'convert' more casual book browsers into buyers.
- Use relevant keyword so that people searching Amazon or Google will see your book high in the search results. Don't forget keywords either when you pick your book title.

What Is Kindle Direct Publishing?

You can publish e-books for free with Kindle Direct Publishing (KDP) and reach millions of readers on Amazon. Publishing is fairly easy and straightforward— according to Amazon it should take you less than 5 minutes and your book appears on Kindle stores worldwide within 24–48 hours.

Amazon says that authors can earn up to 70% royalty of sales. Note that is 'can' and royalties can vary, depending on aspects such as location. If you enrol in KDP Select there is the potential to earn more money through Kindle Unlimited and the Kindle Owners' Lending Library.

With Kindle Direct Publishing, you keep control of your rights and set your own list prices. You can also make changes to your books at any time.

Some things to consider with KDP:

- Unlike most other digital retailers, KDP previously used the format known as MOBI. This was the file format for digital books that Amazon used but they now use EPUB format.
- You can upload your book on Amazon in various formats, including EPUB, which is the most popular one (what Apple uses), and others such as HTML, Doc, and RTF.
- If you have written your book in Word and want to convert it to EPUB, you can do this using the free software Calibre (available for PC or Mac).
- Another option is to pay digital publishing or formatting companies that offer the service of converting a Word file to the digital format of your choice.

ISBN

9

Every book is issued an International Standard Book Number (ISBN).

Before it was implemented in 1967, the method and system for cataloguing, ordering, organising, and locating a specific book was chaotic. Today, to get your book into a bookstore, a library, or almost any book distribution channel on the planet, you need an ISBN. As of 2007, the ISBN is a 13-digit number. This came about in part because of the large volume of e-books now being published every year.

You can only use an ISBN once. The ISBN is a unique number for that particular book, and can be assigned once, and only once, to that title. It can't be used with any other book in the future, even second versions of the same book.

You don't need an ISBN to sell in each individual country. ISBNs are international; they are just assigned locally. A US-based publisher can purchase their ISBN through Bowker but can stock their book worldwide using that ISBN.

You need an ISBN for every specific format of the book and any new versions. Want to sell your book in print, as an e-book, and also as an audiobook? That's great; however, you need a different ISBN for each one. If you want to publish a revised and updated version, you'll also need a new ISBN. (This doesn't cover fixing some typos and errors.)

If you create a series of books you can't use the same ISBN for them. You can use the same ISSN, however. Many fiction and non-fiction authors have an ISSN number assigned to their book series. ISSN stands for International Standard Series Number; however, each book in the series will need its own ISBN.

ASIN

Amazon's Kindle Direct Publishing (KDP) uses ASIN. ASIN numbers are used by Amazon to manage and identify the products they are selling on their site. It's a 10-character alphanumeric unique identifier that's assigned by ▶ Amazon.com and its partners.

An ASIN is not the same as an ISBN. You can only use it with Amazon. If you want to sell through other platforms or in brick-and-mortar stores, you also need an ISBN.

Do You Need an ISBN?

If you want to publish and sell your e-book on Amazon, then the quick answer is no, it isn't necessary. Amazon will assign your e-book an ASIN number which will be used to identify and track your title. However, that's only with Amazon, and only with e-books. If you want your readers to get a hold of a print version of your book, then you're going to need an ISBN. If you want to sell your book by means other than as an e-book on Amazon, then you'll need an ISBN.

Free or Paid ISBN?

Self-published authors can get assigned a free ISBN by KDP. If you obtain a free ISBN from another company (or distributor like Smashwords or Apple), those companies will be listed as the publisher. You can also get an ISBN when dealing with a whole host of On-Demand or self-publishing companies like Draft2Digital, Smashwords, or IngramSpark.

BUT: most of the time, you can only use those free ISBNs with the channels those companies distribute through. If you go with different distribution channels you can end up with multiple ISBNs for the same book.

Buy ISBN

You can buy ISBNs directly from Nielsen Bookdata (UK) and Bowker (US). With a purchased ISBN, the author has control of the data, meaning the author can list themselves or their publishing company as the publisher. By buying your ISBN directly you become the publishers of the record and have that extra control.

▶ https://www.isbn.nielsenbookdata.co.uk

Barcode

The barcode isn't the same as the ISBN and when you purchase an ISBN you don't automatically get a barcode. The barcode of your book can change, while your ISBN can remain the same.

A book barcode goes on the back cover of your book. Two numbers are encoded in the book barcode: the ISBN and the price (and the currency it's being sold in). Barcodes are a necessary element of your book as they allow for most retailers and distributors to scan your ISBN for retail and inventory reasons. The standard barcode is known as the EAN (European Article Number) barcode, and your barcode must be in this format to sell your book in bookstores.

Obtaining your e-book barcode:
- First you'll need to decide whether to encode your retail price.
- If you choose to encode your price, you'll decide what the five digits will be in the five-digit price add-on. The first digit is the currency indicator.
- If you choose not to encode your retail price, the add-on is 90,000. This indicates there is no data encoded.
- A free barcode is included on any cover template from print-on-demand printers such as Amazon KDP and IngramSpark.

▶ https://www.createbarcodes.com/

? EXERCISE 9.1: Amazon Research

Go onto Amazon and look up some of your favourite authors.
- What do you like/dislike about their Amazon bios?
- Compare some bios from different authors
  – What information do they include?
  – How long are their bios?
- Do they have a photo?

9

? EXERCISE 9.2: Produce Your Cover

In Exercise 8.2 we produced a design brief for our covers. Now we're going to turn that brief into reality. With some help to make it easier.
Steps:
1. Go to Canva: ▶ www.canva.com
2. In the search bar, type in book cover
3. Now page through the list of covers and see if you can find one that you think is appealing and seems a reasonable fit to your design brief. Remember that you can change most aspects—such as cover, fonts, and images—and you can delete aspects. So this is just the starting point.
4. Now you can customise the cover so that it meets your design brief.

Your E-book Marketing Strategy

Contents

© The Author(s), under exclusive license to Springer Nature Switzerland AG 2023
L. Kesteven, *Publishing Online for Writers*,
https://doi.org/10.1007/978-3-031-21366-3_10

About this Chapter

In this chapter we will:

- Understand why having an e-book marketing strategy is important
- Consider the different components of an e-book marketing strategy
- Discuss how to launch your e-book: Pricing, publication date, and promotion
- Consider using social media and other channels
- EXERCISES: (1) Theme and Audience and (2) What's your Genre?
- CHECKLIST: E-book Marketing Strategy

Having your e-book published online is only the start. Many writers stop here and wonder why their e-book doesn't sell in the volume they'd hoped. To be successful, any author needs to consider many aspects of e-book marketing, which will be covered in this chapter.

The Importance of Having a Marketing Strategy for your E-book

If you had gone down the traditional book route and published your book via a publisher, then it's possible they would advise you on a marketing strategy. Why do they do this? It's very simple—your book won't sell itself. With so many books out there, vying for the attention of potential readers, without a marketing strategy your e-book just don't get noticed.

I've attended many conferences aimed at writers over the years, and one thing that has always stood out to me was the number of authors who said they have been published but then added that they hadn't sold many copies. And as self-publishing has become more and more popular (not surprising with the difficulty in getting the attention of agents and publishers) the number of self-published authors with few sales is only increasing. So unless you want to be an author with few sales, then having an e-book marketing strategy that you implement is a must have, not a nice to have.

So, what's the purpose of an e-book marketing strategy? It's to generate sales and build your reputation as an author. While generating interest is great, that's only useful if that interest turns into a sale.

And remember, e-book marketing isn't just about your e-book. Think about books that sell well today—do you know who the author is? It's very unlikely that we wouldn't. That's because any book that is sold today is part of a brand, and that brand includes the author.

If an e-book marketing strategy is so important then why don't more authors have one? Because it takes research, time, and effort. Those authors that I know who do this very well all say that it can be a full-time job at times. If you've got a budget, then it's something you could outsource to an e-book marketing expert. But if that's not an option then it is something that you can do yourself—and with careful planning, it's well worth the effort. And with a good plan, you can ensure your time is well spent.

Contents of Your E-book Marketing Strategy

Your marketing strategy will likely contain the following:
- Marketing budget
- Time allocated to marketing
- Your field
- Your target audience
- Promotional activities
  - Website
  - Blog
  - Social media
  - Pre-launch
- Advertising
- Deciding what to charge

Decide Your Marketing Budget

Do you have enough money to market your e-book? Even if your budget is very small or non-existent, you can still market your book with self-promotion, but if you can manage it, even a small budget can help you further your exposure. And depending on your skill set, it might be worth spending your budget in areas where you're not confident. For example, if design isn't your thing, then spending your budget on getting a professional cover would be well worth it.

Some aspects that you might want to spend your marketing budget on:
- Support producing your manuscript. Not everyone has the necessary technical skills to produce the required files ready for online production, so if it's not your expertise that shouldn't stop you from publishing your e-book. They are companies available that can deliver all the steps you need (at a price) or you can select the services you want.
- Design factors—Such as your cover or promotional material for social media.
- Advertising—There are advertising packages available (e.g., Amazon offers various packages for authors).
- Marketing advice—If some of the activities below start to look a bit overwhelming, don't despair. There are experts available who can help you (provided you have the funds).
- Promotion activities—Just because your e-book is online that doesn't mean you can't have a launch event.
- Social media support—Again, social media isn't everyone's cup of tea, and I know from personal experience that it can be a real-time consumer! So, if you can afford to, it's not a bad approach to outsource this to someone. In the past, I've relied on a young person (who was keen to make some part-time income) who was very social media savvy—they'd spend 2–3 hours a week on social media for my work—and I was impressed with how much they achieved.

How Much Time Do You Really Have to Put Aside for Marketing?

Now comes the bad news—good marketing takes time. If you think sending out a few emails once a month is going to cut it, then I'm afraid you're going to be disappointed.

If you're looking after marketing yourself, then realistically you need to set time aside at least 2–3 hours a week ongoing. And to get everything setup (think website, profiles, etc.) allows yourself at least a week, potentially two. It will take you more time initially, but as you become more familiar with marketing, it will take you less time.

Don't forget, if you went down the traditional route of publishing your work with a publishing house, then they would have a marketing team providing marketing services (this is one of the reasons the publishing house takes a share of the profits from the sale of your book). So, if you're going to self publish, then you need to replace this effort—either by outsourcing it or by doing it yourself.

Understand Your Field or Sector

To begin with, you'll need to research your sector and understand how it ticks. It's very likely that your field has established routes—let's say it's an academic book on a particular subject. While you can promote it on your website, unless you're a recognised authority in your field and your website is well known, then you'll only reach a very limited audience. But perhaps there are industry blogs available that you could write a blog post for. Perhaps there are magazines they like to read.

It's good to get to know your typical reader. Where do they like to hang out (online)? Is there a particular format or medium they prefer? Are there websites that review books in your particular genre?

Who Is Your Target Audience?

To determine how best to market your e-book, you'll need to identify who you are marketing it to. It might seem easier to just say—I just want to reach everyone—but this isn't going to cut it and, through a lack of focus, you'll reach no one.

By focusing your marketing efforts on the group that will be interested in your work, you have a great chance of converting that interest into sales. It will also allow you to create a strategy that works best for them and your e-book.

Let's say your target audience is young adults—you'd take a very different strategy then if your book was an historical fiction on World War II and you were targeting a middle-aged audience. Using my young adult example, I'd need to think about where young adults go for book recommendations. I bet it would be a very different source than my middle-aged audience interested in WWII fiction.

Connect with Your Potential Reader

To make a connection you need to tell your readers why they would be interested in your e-book and how they will benefit from reading it. Let's say my novel is aimed at young adults and perhaps it includes themes such as relationships or bullying or gender identity (just a few examples). By sharing with your potential readership the theme of your work, there's the chance you'll build a connection and they'll want to read your work because it's a theme that resonates with them.

Some ways to connect with your audience?
- Websites they frequent
- Blogs they read
- Magazines they read
- Review sites
- Via respected authorities
- Events they attend (such as conferences—not always dry and boring, think comic-con)
- Things they enjoy (games, movies, TV shows, etc.)
- Social media (are they more likely to use Facebook [more likely middle-aged] or Twitter or Instagram ….)

10

Another way you can connect with your reader is to become a recognised authority in the field. Now, this doesn't mean you have to be an expert, so long as you're honest. Many social media influencers aren't experts, but what they do is share their own experiences with say a product. They use relatable and often real-life stories to make a connection between readers and brands. And with social media influencers—this is what they are tapping into. In a world saturated with advertising, it's hardly surprising that we'd rather trust that 'friend' on social media who has tried a product rather than a celebrity that we know has been paid to say it's great.

How Are You Going to Position Your E-book or Work?

It's important to get specific—ending up in a general category is not a good thing. Actually, it's very bad! Think about when you go into a bookstore—would you head to a section that had everything mixed in together on one big table? You really wouldn't know where to begin.

Therefore, you really need to be specific. It's not enough for me to describe my novel as historical fiction—there are just so many sub-categories. The historical fiction reader who enjoys reading about the Tudors may not be interested in the Romans, or the World Wars.

Website Promotion

You have a few options: you might already have an author website and you can showcase your latest e-book on there. Or you might choose to have a dedicated website for your book.

A Landing Page

Regardless of your approach, you're going to want your website visitors to immediately know about your book/latest release. Your landing page needs to capture their attention—it might be with the cover of your book and perhaps a short blurb. You might have some details of your latest activities—let's say you're doing some book promotions at a local bookstore. But what you must have is a link that takes interested website visitors to a place where they can buy your book. You might sell it from your website or you could link it to a marketplace (such as Amazon) and take them directly to your book page.

You'll need to indicate whether your e-book is free or paid and where it can be bought or downloaded. You can also add an overview of your e-book—this might be your blurb but this could potentially be too long for a landing page—so don't be afraid to write a snappy overview for your website. There's also the opportunity to link to other aspects—perhaps you want to offer the first chapter for free, provide background information to your work, or useful links if someone is interested in a particular theme. My advice on the 'free' content is it needs to be part of a strategy. If giving away one chapter results in purchases on your e-book, that's great. But don't put a lot of valuable content online if it's unlikely to bring benefit either to your 'brand' or your e-book sales.

Assess Your Website and Landing Page

In order to get a good conversion rate from your landing page, you need to make sure your landing page is well optimised. What do I mean by this? I'm not going to get too technical but it means that you need to understand if your website is working for you:

- Get to know your website and assess aspects such as the site navigation, context, and overall cosmetics of the website. See if there are any issues. For example, perhaps there is a specific page that doesn't get much site traffic (or visitors)—that's a strong indicator that you need to improve that page or your navigation isn't great (maybe the page isn't easily accessible). Once you've determined common issues (e.g., lack of site traffic on a specific page), you can proceed.
- It can be other aspects too—such as your domain name—if it has no connection to you as an author or your work, then that might be an issue.
- Check out your competitors and evaluate how your website stacks up against theirs. I'm certainly not suggesting that you imitate them, but it's good to understand what's happening in your space and how you might compare.
- Keywords. These are words or terms that relate to your site's content.

Blog

Now that you have a website with a WOW landing page which is immediately going to tell your visitor about your new e-book, you'll need to work on supporting content. An image is great to capture attention, but sometimes readers want to find out more. This is where you can provide supporting content which enables you to really connect with your potential reader. This is where a blog can really provide value. By creating a blog, you not only get a chance to display your writing skills, but also engage with potential readers and drive traffic to your landing page.

Some blog posts you might want to consider:
- Themes that resonate in your book
- Your research
- Your writing practices

Connect with your potential reader's pain points. Maybe they're aware that there is a real driver to find out more about amazing women from history.

Website Content

Now's the time to get creative with content that a reader of your book might be interested in.

This could include:
- A preview—just a snippet to catch their attention.
- Any information that relates to the content in your e-book.
- Some interesting details about aspects of your e-book. Let's say you're writing about a particular period in time. You might want to share some interesting aspects of your research that is touched upon in your writing.
- Maybe your reader wants to know more. You could give them additional information or links to where they can find out more.

Your writing process. What inspires you? I have an author friend who writes about amazing women from history. She shares stories about other inspiring women she comes across, not just the ones she's written about.

Videos

Videos can also be a part of your marketing strategy. Videos that are quick to watch and are appealing are a great way of reaching out to potential audiences. That said, they need to appear professional—and by that, I mean a self-recording video you've made yourself on your phone is unlikely to cut it. That doesn't mean that you can't make them yourself, but you need to invest the time to ensure it's well made. Informal is okay—if you look on Instagram there are plenty of influencers making their own videos—but they are carefully thought out, likely researched, and well prepared and produced.

Guest Blogging

Guest blogging is a popular method used by authors to promote an e-books and is a great way to build your reputation and authority in your field. But it is also a means to increase your reach to others who might be interested in your e-book. Where can you guest blog? You'll need to do your research and find suitable sites that have some connection to your e-book.

You want to be associated with blogs and websites that appeal to a similar audience as yours. Read through blogs that could relate to your e-book and see if they can benefit from your knowledge or expertise. Often, it's best to approach this as a partnership—maybe the blog belongs to an author who works in a similar field, so there might be the opportunity to promote each other's work.

This might seem like a lot of work, and I won't dispute it—it is. You need to research and find suitable blogs, use your communication and negotiation skills to get the blogger on board, and then potentially write posts. But remember this is marketing that you won't need to pay for—some coming back to what we discussed at the beginning. What you're not spending in money, you're putting in as your time.

What are the benefits of guest blogging? It allows you to reach an audience that might otherwise not know about you and your e-book, it helps to build your brand and reputation, and it helps grow your network.

And while we're discussing guest blogging, this works both ways. Find bloggers with a connection and invite them to write a post for your blog.

Paid Advertising?

Knowing how to promote your e-book online strategically and creatively is crucial. That said, sometimes you need to put some money behind your content to get sufficient traffic. So, it is work setting aside a budget for paid advertising and consider running campaigns on LinkedIn, Google, or Facebook.

Pre-launch Promotions

So, you've written your e-book, produced your manuscript, and have found the platform to launch it. Before you take that step, there are some marketing steps that will help you make the most of this important event.

Pre-launch marketing, done well, builds excitement with your prospective customers by sharing sneak peeks of your e-book. You might consider sharing with them the production phase of your e-book to build that connection.

You've already created the landing page, so you can use that same page for your pre-launch activities too. This might include sharing your cover and maybe you would want to have an offer for those that purchase your e-book ahead of its launch. If you can provide a way for visitors to your website to leave an email, you can keep in touch and let them know about the launch.

Another way of building up excitement ahead of launch is to run some kind of promotion. It might be something as simple as voting for your e-book title or cover.

Social Media as Part of Your E-book Marketing Strategy

You can promote your e-book on various social platforms such as Facebook, Twitter, LinkedIn, Pinterest, Instagram, TikTok, and YouTube. Many writers utilise social media as an important component of their marketing strategy—to promote their e-book but also to promote themselves as a writer.

Online platforms allow you to connect with your audience and potential readers. This connection is often on a more personal level where you can engage and interact with your audience.

This first step is to make yourself visible on social media. If people need to search to find you, they probably won't bother. By being visible, not only does this make you seem accessible but it also builds your credibility and expertise. Readers love to be able to contact you directly—but be warned, they are just as likely to have complaints as well as questions. So you'll need to decide if this is a path you want to go down. As much as it's a great way to build a connection, it can also be a huge time consumer, and not to mention, a way to harm your fledgling confidence (especially if it's your first time publishing a book). So, a carefully thought-out approach is essential.

The main advantage of using social media is that it can be used 24/7, with social media sites available on any device at any time. But that doesn't mean you should overdo it. Too many posts and people will potentially unfollow you because you're annoying.

Top tip: Keep it short regardless of the social media platform. People rarely read for extended amounts of time using a digital device.

Social Media Posts Can Include:

- Visuals of your e-book—show your potential reader the cover so they don't forget it
- Interesting facts about your e-book and any related themes
- Your writing process and any tips
- Short how to guides
- Build up interest and anticipation for an upcoming release date

- Quotes from your e-book
- Events related to your e-book and any related themes

Have a Theme

Followers enjoy following a journey. I have a writer friend who is just about to have her first book published and she shared each step of her journey via social media.

Your theme might be an upcoming e-book launch. Give your followers something special and make them feel like they are a part of a special group. You might share some of your research or what drove you to write about your topic. Perhaps people have been asking questions and you could share these.

Decide Which Social Media Platforms to Use

You can go with them all but do so with caution! Social media and keeping yourself visible with regular posts can chew up a lot of time. Best to start slow; select one and see how you go. If you have enough time, then add another. Which one to go with? Find the platform that your target audience prefers.

Promote Your E-Book via Email Marketing

I don't know about you, but I pretty much skim emails at most, and if any have a whiff of being a scam, I swiftly delete it. But, done well, there is research that says it can still work. Just take your time to prepare it well to avoid the trash can:

- Have an attention-grabbing subject line that encourages the reader to keep going
- Bullet points are great and much easier to read
- There needs to be a call to action
- Give the recipient something—perhaps it's a discount, the first chapter of your e-book

Launch an Email Outreach Programme

An outreach programme is when you try to contact key people related to your industry. For example, they might be influencers, bloggers, authors, or interviewers. The aim is to gain exposure for your new e-book by their promotion. An email outreach programme can connect you with people who want to collaborate. But it will take some work. It's unlikely that you can simply send them an email and they'll jump at the opportunity to work with you. You'll need to convince them that you have something to offer to them - What's in it for them! Perhaps they have a particular interest in the theme of your work. It helps if you're not a stranger; for example, you might be a follower on their twitter account and have responded on occasion to something they've posted. What's important is that you need to stand out. If they're good at what they do, and have a reasonable number of followers, then they'll get approached frequently. So you need to be able to sell yourself and your work and convince them why they should promote it. Their aim is to build relationships with other professionals in your industry. Over time, these connections can lead to partnerships or interviews that directly promote your e-book.

What to Charge

E-books are high-volume, low-sales-price offers. This means you'll need to sell a lot of them at a relatively low price point in order to compete in the digital book marketplace and turn a significant profit. Depending on your industry, e-books can range from free to more than $100.

Before setting a price for your e-book, do some research. Determine who your audience is, what they're willing to pay, and how many people within your target market might be willing to buy it. Then, determine the platforms you'll sell your e-book through. Amazon? Apple Books? Your own website? You can research how much e-books usually go for on these sites and incorporate this insight into your pricing strategy.

It should not be too expensive. E-books should be reasonably priced to be competitive.

10

Coordinating Your Marketing Activities

If you want to make your e-book release more impactful, consider when it is best to time to launch. Some examples might be if your e-book is a typical 'summer read' that you might want to time it for summer (remember though, summer will change depending where on the global you're marketing your e-book). Maybe it's connected with an anniversary—perhaps your e-book is set during WWI and there's a significant anniversary coming up. Leveraging these events helps to increase visibility on your e-book and it's an easy way to get your e-book to a wider audience.

Track, Measure, and Refine Your Strategy

If you're going to invest effort, time, and potentially money in your marketing strategy, it is important to assess whether it is working. This will give you useful insights so you can decide what marketing efforts work for you and where any changes are needed.

Ways to measure your marketing strategy:
- Track both outbound and internal activity on your e-book page.
- After each marketing event, analyse any statistics you can obtain (e.g., you can collate your Amazon views and sales).
- Look for any trends that show your event is working.

❓ EXERCISE 10.1: Theme and Audience

Steps:

1. List all the themes that are prevalent in your book.
2. Now decide who is your target audience.
3. For each theme, consider why your target audience would be interested.
4. How could you further refine your theme to make it more relevant to your target audience?
5. What are some ways you could connect with your target audience?

❓ EXERCISE 10.2: What's Your Genre?

If your work isn't a novel, then instead of genre use topic or theme.

Steps:

1. What is your genre or topic/theme?
2. How to try and narrow it down further? Is there a sub-genre or sub-category that it would fit into?
3. Now see if you can narrow it down even further. You'd be surprised how many sub-categories there can be. Don't be shy to go online and do some research into your genre/category.

■ **CHECKLIST: E-book Marketing Strategy**

Budget	How much can you afford to spend on marketing your e-book?
Time	How much of your own time can you realistically invest in marketing your e-book?
Field	What is your field?
Target audience	Which readers are you hoping to reach?
Promotional activities	Which of the following will you use to promote your e-book: • Website • Blogs • Social media • Other
Pre-launch activities	What activities will you perform to prepare for the launch of your e-book? (► Chapter 11 will explore different promotional activities for marketing e-books)
Monitoring	How will you monitor if your marketing strategy is working well?

Promoting Your E-book

Contents

© The Author(s), under exclusive license to Springer Nature
Switzerland AG 2023
L. Kesteven, *Publishing Online for Writers*,
https://doi.org/10.1007/978-3-031-21366-3_11

About this Chapter

In this chapter we will:
- Explore different ways to promote your work
- Consider how to use social media to your advantage
- Discuss pitfalls to avoid
- EXERCISE: Design your Launch Campaign

The self-published author very quickly realises that it's very unlikely, actually it's far more likely impossible, for their book to get noticed amongst the huge volume of other self-publications without promotion. Therefore, promotions are key and help turn your marketing strategy into reality.

The obvious benefit of promoting your book yourself—versus paid promotion—is that you'll save a lot of money. The downside is that what you save in money you'll need to make up for with your time. But even if you have a budget for advertising and marketing, self-promotion is another means to gain further exposure. Exposure means more people know about your work, which will hopefully result in further sales. But equally important is that more people know about you as an author and your work.

Promotion isn't just about your e-book or work—if you're serious about building a career as an author, then you're also promoting yourself as a writer. Self-promoting your book helps build connections, both with any existing audience, but it also allows you to make new connections. These could be readers, but they might also be reviewers, other authors, agents, and publishers. Such connections are invaluable as you move forward in your career as an author.

In this chapter we'll explore different ways to promote your work, with many of these utilising social media.

11

Promoting Your E-book

Reviews

Reviews are essential if you want to sell your e-book in significant volumes. It's quite common for people to want to see what previous readers thought before committing to buying. I know that I'll often have a quick skim through reviews when I'm looking at a book on Amazon or GoodReads. Do I believe them all? No, I don't. Of course, everyone has different tastes when it comes to books. But if there's enough reviews it can give you a sense of the type of book.

So, as a new author, where do you get reviews? Send the book to people in the industry or experts in the topic covered in the book, co-workers, friends, and family … then ask them to submit an honest review. People do need to be prompted sometimes, so if you get some nice feedback on your work, ask the person if they would be willing to write you a review. Where should they write their reviews? There are various options, but Amazon is probably one of the most read book review sites. And the great thing about Amazon is that it recommends other writers like you, so you can see who they are and they can see you. This is no bad thing because writers tend to be readers too; I know I am.

There will be magazines and journals that have book review sections, and you can sometimes approach them with your e-book. Again, check their websites for contact details.

And while we're on the subject of reviews:

- Right after the last chapter, it's an opportunity to thank the reader for reading your book and politely ask for a review.
- Make it easy for them to write a review by linking to the e-book page on your retailer's website (e.g., the e-book page at Amazon, if that's you've listed your book).

Offer a Teaser

Social media teasers are a way to generate awareness and interest in your e-book, as well giving potential readers an incentive to part with their money. By providing potential readers with a glimpse of what your e-book is about, you're hopefully tempting them to find out more. A teaser could be a sample chapter, or it might be something else—perhaps it's a short video about it, some information that sets the scene—the trick is to entice and draw your readers in. It can help build a sense of excitement and anticipation about what's to come. If your e-book is just being launched and you need some early readers, give them an incentive with a discount.

It's quite common to find the first chapter of another e-book (might be the next one in the series or another book by the same author) at the end of a book/e-book. It's a way of capturing your reader's attention at an important moment. If they've enjoyed the book they will be keen to read on, to know more, if it's one of a series. Even if it's not, I'll often give it a try just to see if I might like it. Always useful to include a link, so if the reader does want to keep reading, it's just a few clicks away.

Find Influencers

Another e-book promotion technique is to leverage the status of a popular individual in their niche to promote your e-book. Do your research and find some relevant influencers. The obvious one is to find influencers that review books in your genre. You might be able to offer them your book to review and hope they'll like it and give you positive reviews. It's also possible that you can find influencers in other fields. There will need to be some relevance—but what's important is that they can reach your target audience. A good example of this one would be someone who is a social media influencer in the field of fantasy games and you write fantasy novels. It's likely that people who are interested in fantasy games are also interested in reading fantasy novels.

The effectiveness of influencer marketing is growing and while some want a commission, this is likely to be less than what is paid in traditional advertising. These influencers, by sharing your e-book with their strong following on different social media platforms, also help build credibility and trust for your e-book.

Creating a Buzz

It's all about stirring up some interest. Think about when a local store might open up in your area. Maybe it's a small cafe, a restaurant, or a bookstore. They're not just going to hope that people will pass by and drop in (let's face it, that's not going to generate much foot fall!). What's more likely is that they will try to generate a buzz about their business. In the past, they might have put out leaflets in local letterboxes or taken out an ad in the local newspaper. I've seen some businesses hire someone to dress up in a crazy costume and handout flyers to passers-by. They'd often offer some promotion—drop in during their first opening week and receive a 10% discount. It's all about encouraging people to step over the threshold and see what's inside. Well, it's no different to creating a buzz about your e-book.

Today, social media has provided us with a very cheap and easy way to get the word out there. We can post advertisements on Facebook, tweet about an upcoming launch event on Twitter, post photos on Instagram about someone who's excited about the upcoming launch party, even offer a special discount via the author's website. Over the week leading up to the launch, you might contact interested parties via an email list that you've collected—say from your website (remember to only email people that have expressed interest in being kept informed about your e-book). But you can also widen your reach by joining forums related to the topic of your work. You might decide to join a Facebookdiscussion and casually mention your work. You might comment on blogs in a related niche with links back to your book website or Amazon page. These activities, on their own, are just small promotions and on their own probably wouldn't generate much interest. But done together in a well-managed and coordinated campaign, people will start to notice.

Online Advertisements

It's easy enough to create your own advertisement (remember Canva that I mentioned earlier? They have advertisement templates that you can tailor). Keep it simple—especially if you want to post it on a social media platform such as Twitter. Make it attractive, not too busy, with just the essential details.

Another option is to run ads though Amazon's AMS program. Launched in 2012, AMS is an advertising platform that allows you to get any product, including e-books featured on Amazon's online store. Such as with any advertising, this can help with brand awareness and product visibility, and hopefully increasing your sales. How does it work? Someone does a keyword search on Amazon and, if it's relevant, it will show an ad for your e-book (e.g., if someone is searching for an e-book in a similar genre they might see an ad for yours). This is a very powerful tool to show your e-book to people who are most likely to be interested.

Pre-launch E-book Promotions

It's often at the point where we're about to launch our e-book that we do the most promotions, but actually it's something that we should be doing regularly and consistently if we want the e-book to continue to sell. But for the moment, let's focus on pre-launch.

Share Your E-book Writing Journey

There are a lot of e-books out there, and one way to capture attention is to establish yourself as a read-worthy author. You, the author, are a brand. And this brand promotes you as an expert writer with a reputation of producing e-books that readers love to read. You can do this by posting useful, inspirational content. Your blog posts, website posts, and social media posts (LinkedIn, Facebook, Twitter, Pinterest, etc.) should reflect your passion for writing and imagination (fiction) or helping people solve certain problems (non-fiction).

Social media can be a powerful promoting tool if you create engaging posts your readers will want to re-post and share. Think about making your inspirational thoughts into quotes or change expert advice into useful tips and shortlists.

Share your beginning steps. Post about your intention to write a book, topic, and the idea, and ask for feedback. If you haven't yet started writing, or you're just outlining your book, your readers' online feedback can both spark interest and provide useful insight into their content needs and preferences.

Give Updates on Your Progress

Are you interviewing experts or visiting interesting places to research for your book? Don't forget to update your audience! Share posts, pictures, and videos so your readers know you're working really hard to create valuable content for them.

Polish Your E-book Cover

Readers judge books by their covers. If you're cover isn't appealing, readers will move on. It's interesting to see how genres will have 'typical' covers—while this can seem frustrating as a writer, when we want to make our cover stand out from the crowd, it's important to realise that readers want to 'recognise' genres that they like.

Remember that e-book design we produced in ▶ Chap. 8? Here is where we can come back and polish our e-book cover to perfection.

Email Lists

You can only email someone if they have provided you with their email address and indicated that they are happy to receive emails from you. If you start trying to email people who haven't given you permission, depending on where you're located, you could find yourself in hot water—but in any case, these days people receive far too many emails and don't appreciate emails they didn't request.

You've probably noticed that online businesses today will often give you an incentive to go onto their mailing lists. A good example of this is giving you a discount for your first purchase. In a similar manner, you could give your email subscribers an incentive—perhaps a discount to use during the first week of launch, a sample from the book, or an invitation to the launch.

Once a significant number of people are on your mailing list, there are various things that you can email them about:

- Send updates on your e-book—for example, publishing date
- Details on where to purchase
- Reviews and relevant posts

Get Involved in a Group Promotion

This is where you join with a group of authors who have books in the same genre or with a similar theme/topic. By working together as a group, each member can email their own email lists, extending your reach.

11

Build Relationships

Sometimes you can work with other websites and businesses that are involved with work relevant to your theme or topic. If there are interested in your work, they will often review it and share it with their followers. This doesn't come easily—you'll probably need to pitch your e-book/work to them and potentially offer something in return (perhaps you can provide a review of their product/s).

Facebook Groups

Another way to spread the work about your e-book is to join relevant Facebook groups. And when I say relevant, this is very important. If the group senses that you've only joined to plug your book, they'll quickly let you know that your presence isn't welcome! But if you can engage in quality discussions and offer something useful (such as information), then they'll potentially be interested in your work. But this is something that takes time and energy—much like your friendship groups—if you only turn up to promote your book then you'll find your friendship circle shrinking! You'll need to build trust and be viewed as someone who contributes politely with unique insights and useful advice. Always keep it professional and don't engage in arguments; this will only be detrimental to your online reputation.

Competitions

I've noticed this has become more and more popular on Instagram with authors offering a free book via an online competition (sometimes this is nothing more than following the person and sharing it with someone else). You could have a competition that offers a free download of your e-book or perhaps signed copies if you're going to be doing some printed versions.

Promotions Using Different Social Media Platforms

Promote Your E-book on Facebook

Here are some ideas for promoting your e-book on Facebook:
- Create an author page
- Link your landing page to your Facebook posts
- Promote via Facebook Ads
- Post about events, reviews, and feedback
- Post about a giveaway or special promotion

Promote Your E-book on Twitter

Twitter is another platform you can utilise as part of your strategy
- Tweet about any upcoming events
- Use images—a picture of the e-book launch, reviews—better to go with images than too much text
- Search relevant keywords for your e-book and find out who is tweeting about it.

Promote Your E-book on Instagram

You can use Instagram as a platform to create a community around your e-book:
- Post about your e-book and anything associated about it—your writing process, e-book events, reviews etc
- Don't forget your bio
- Again, images are great—don't write out the review—take a photo of it and post it
- Share something from your e-book—photo of the black blurb

Promote Your E-book on YouTube

YouTube is another channel to reach more customers. You can:
- Upload videos titled around relevant topics and link your e-book as a source of more beneficial information
- Post slideshows, how-to videos, or Q&A videos to share valuable information
- Create a short book advertisement that showcases your book cover and any call-to-action at the beginning or end of your video
- Post a video of you (or someone) doing a reading of a 'good bit'

Free Online E-book Advertising

Contact Book Reviewers   There are book reviewers out there—many of them on social media and engaging with them is a great bit of promotion. There are also e-book reviewers who will provide a review in exchange for a free copy. These aren't just people who are avid readers; many are authors who have a following and share with their audience books they enjoy. It's a form of collaboration that is great for all parties involved—but remember it's important to give as well as take, so doing some reviews yourself is a great thing to do.

Guest Blog Posts   I've mentioned these in an earlier chapter, and I'm raising them again because they are a very effective way of promotion.

Podcasts and Interviews   Interviews of all kinds—whether blogs, videos, or podcasts—are great forums for having your e-book discussed in some depth as well as presenting yourself to future readers. Being on a podcast helps readers perceive you as someone who is well-informed on the topic and has something useful to offer. You can use podcasts to share your opinions on a certain topic but also give free instructions and strategies that can be further explored in your book.

Online Bookstores and Websites   This will need some research, but you will find online bookstores and websites (some targeting specific genres) that are interested in promoting books.

❷ **EXERCISE 11: Design Your Launch Campaign**

Let's assume you've completed your work, uploaded it to an e-book platform, and have the file/s ready to send off to your chosen e-book retailer. From the activities listed about—and any others that you might like to include—come with a list of ten activities that you'll run in the week leading up to your launch. The table below should help with your planning. I've included the first one to get you started (feel free to delete it if it's not suitable).

Activity	Platform	When
Post an image of the e-book cover with details of the online launch	Instagram	1 week prior to launch

Publishing Online: Making It a Success

Contents

An Online Writer's Website

Contents

© The Author(s), under exclusive license to Springer Nature
Switzerland AG 2023
L. Kesteven, *Publishing Online for Writers*,
https://doi.org/10.1007/978-3-031-21366-3_12

About this Chapter

In this chapter we will:
- Consider how an author can use a website to their advantage
- Explore useful resources
- Discuss pitfalls to avoid
- EXERCISE: Author Brands
- CHECKLIST: Your Author Website

Many authors have various social media channels, and websites are a popular choice. If you're self-published, the responsibility of building (or at least getting one built) falls to the writer. In this chapter, we'll look at what aspects a writer should consider for their e-book website and what's available to help fast track the process.

Does an Author Need a Website?

I'm afraid this one isn't really negotiable. If you want to come across as a professional author, then you need a website. You will see in this chapter that author websites come in all different ways, some providing lots of information and options to interact, others are more like a brochure. But in today's market, a website is something that readers expect. If you don't have one, it's possible they will decide you're not a serious writer. Just like any product, service or person we are engaging with, often the first step we take is to do an internet search!

But before you start crying in your porridge at the prospect of having and maintaining a website, there are ways to make it easier and not too onerous.

Your Author Platform

A website is the platform you can wave to everyone from. It's a way to make yourself seen, a place for you to put yourself forward as a writer and because it's YOURS you can decide how you want to promote yourself and your work. It's where many people will come to find out about you and your work—and that includes agents and publishers, as well as your readers.

The Purpose of an Author Website

Your website will give you:
1. Credibility. It says that you're a serious writer and that you're a professional
2. Visibility. It's a platform to showcase your work
3. Connection. That could be to readers, other authors, publishers, agents—you name it—they can become your followers. Gather their email addresses and you'll have your email list

Getting Started

Choose Your Platform

Your website is built within a platform; many of these are very user friendly with pre-existing templates that you can tailor to suit your needs. They'll often have themes—for example, Wix provides layouts for different professional looks (even some for writers)—you don't have to stick to ones in your theme. I tend to browse through them and see which ones standout and suit the look I'm going for. Wix is a good example of a platform that is very interactive and you can build a website quickly. But there are others: WordPress has been around a long time and very popular. I've also used Blogger. Depending on what you want to do and the features you want, they do provide simple designs that cost little or have no cost.

Select a Domain Host

The domain host is the place where your website will reside. The hosting company owns the hardware that drives your website and you rent your online space from them. They are responsible for making sure your website is available on the internet. They don't own your website and aren't responsible for what you post on it.

Free hosting is available, and these sites often require you to use their address or purchase the domain name from them. In return for free hosting, they may place ads on your website. If you don't like the idea of this, you will need to consider paying for web hosting (I'd recommend you search for this and compare what they offer).

12

Pick a Domain Name

This is your web address or your URL and what is used to bring up your website. One option is to purchase this through your hosting site, and this is often the cheapest option. The downside of this is that the URL is typically longer and not necessarily as you want it.

The other option is to spend more and get the domain name that you like—if it's available. If it's not, you might have to be flexible and choose a different extension (such as .net rather than .com).

What's a Good Domain Name?

Keep it relevant. Keep it simple. Keep it memorable. Keep it professional. Simply your ▶ name.com (▶ Jane.Jones.com, or as I have often seen ▶ JaneJones.Writer. com)—simple, honest and to the point.

Remember your email address is something that you'll need to regularly give out, so if you make it complicated, you're going to regret it.

Add Domain Security

When you purchase a domain name, ICANN (The Internet Corporation for Assigned Names and Numbers) requires that you provide your personal contact information, making it publicly available. When you purchase domain security, a third party becomes the owner, thus protecting your personal information by taking over as landlord. Some hosts offer Domain Privacy Protection which is worth considering.

Build and Design Your Author Website Yourself

Avoid the temptation to settle for one of the quick and easy website designs that look like everyone else's, giving it a small-time feel. Creating your own great-looking custom site has become easier and cheaper than ever. What's important is that the design reflects the image that you want to portray—so those decisions you made of the design of your e-book might also become useful with your website.

If, however, you simply don't want the hassle, and your budget allows it, hire someone to do it.

Design tip: Many people browse the internet on their phone, so make sure your design is mobile phone friendly.

Know Your Audience

You already have this information if you have prepared your marketing strategy (see ► Chap. 10). Just like with your e-book, it's important to bear in mind who your audience are and what they might expect from your website.

Audiences can differ and have different expectations—for example, if you write fantasy novels that have many characters and complex worlds, readers can seek out the author's website for further information. It's not uncommon in this genre for authors to provide a page dedicated to the fantasy world and their characters.

If it's non-fiction, readers can be looking for more information, perhaps the research behind the work or a blog where the author provides further exploration of ideas and themes.

But your typical readership will also affect how you design your website. For example, if your e-book is for a young adult readership, it will have a different approach than say, one aimed for a middle-aged readership.

Pages to Include on Your Website

Typically, a website will have a homepage with a menu that takes you to further pages. For ease of navigation, try to keep your menu simple and uncluttered. This will help visitors to your website quickly find their way around.

The area at the top of your website is key and typically includes a header that identifies you. You might also have a tagline that describes you or you might like to include a short quote that someone has used to describe you.

The Homepage

The homepage is the landing page and the first page that the website visitors will see when they land on your site. It's their first impression, so it's worth investing time (and getting design advice if you're not sure about design aspects) to get it right.

The homepage is like the first area you see when you walk into a store. It's often the place where a visitor will decide whether to say or not, so regardless if it's a shop or a website, it needs to be appealing.

A simple design works best, and if you have a suitable image (or two, but don't go overboard), then this can help create the image you want. The content of your homepage should change regularly to reflect what is happening in your author's life. For example, perhaps you have a book launch coming up, or you want to promote a book signing event.

Your website visitor needs to immediately realise that they are at the correct website, so a cover of your e-book would be great. If you're running a promotion, then you need to make this easy for your visitors to find, so your homepage is great for this.

Connections to your other social media sites are great—this means that visitors who want to connect with you further can easily find you on other platforms. Include the links at the bottom of your page. And while we're on the subject of making connections, don't forget that email list you're hoping to compile with people who'd like to find out more about your upcoming e-book—so give them an option to be added to your email list.

About the Author

It's tempting to avoid this page if you're not so keen on promoting yourself, but readers will be curious about you, especially if they enjoy your work. It's up to you how much you share, but remember, you can treat the 'author you' as a persona and very separate from the person that your friends and family know. Very few of us really look like those professional photographs that we have on LinkedIn (or dare I say it, on dating websites). We want to portray an image, so treat this in a simple approach. That said, we all like authors who we can relate to and seem human, so try to have some of your personality come through.

This is the website for Rachel Ivan (▶ http://www.rachelivan.com/) and if you scroll down, you'll come to her 'About the Author' section:

Rachel was born in London but her parents moved to India where her teenage years were spent happily at her grandmother's sprawling house opposite a lake in Bangalore. An avid movie buff, her adoration of travel matches her love for films— she dreams of one day strolling barefoot along a white sandy beach in the Maldives.

The lies we were promised is her first book and was inspired by her frequent trips to India, which she has described as a 'vibrant land of explosive smells, cultures and colours that are a feast for the senses'. Rachel hopes the thought provoking and emotional theme of the story will resonate in the hearts of her readers and remain with them long after the last page has been turned.

She works in the UK Civil Service and lives in South London with her family.

I really like this because it's brief but I immediately feel like I know something about the author even though she's actually revealed very little about herself.

Some tips for this page:

- Focus on yourself as a writer (your readers don't need to know about your personal life).
- Remember anyone can access your website, so don't share any details that you wouldn't want a stranger to know. For example, it might seem harmless to mention your favourite cafe where you grab a coffee every morning, but in the wrong hands, that piece of information could be dangerous.
- Your biography only needs to include the relevant details of your writing and work. You don't need to share your whole life story.
- Short and concise is best; no one probably needs to know what primary school you went to (unless it happens to be relevant).

In reality, it doesn't even need to be true—some authors have written under a pen name with a fictional backstory. I'm not advocating that's a great way to build a connection with your readers but for some authors, it has worked to create their writer persona. Generally, I've found it's far better to be honest but be careful with what you share.

Should You Include a Photograph of Yourself?

Again, this is very much a personal choice. If you're a well-known author, people will recognise you. As I write this book, I've looked up Neil Gaiman's website and he happens to have a photo on his home page: ▶ https://neilgaiman.com/. It looks great and I immediately recognise it as his website because he has such a well-known face in the book world. Interestingly, when I click on the link to his MouseCircus website (for his younger readers), the website has a very different feel. On the first page are images of his books (which his young visitors would hopefully recognise) and his photo is on his Meet Neil Gaiman Page. Take a look if you're interested, but the photograph on this site is quite different to the one on his website for adult readers.

Some people like to see the author of the book they are reading and enjoying—like finding the author's picture on the back sleeve of a printed book. And coming back to the point above about making a connection and coming across as very human and personable—a good quality photograph can really help this.

If you are going to use a photograph:

- Make sure it's professional (if you know someone who's great with taking photos—brilliant, otherwise, it's worth investing in some professional headshots).
- That's right, I just said headshots. If it's a full body shot of you on the beach, no one will really be able to see you. So just like that image you put up on LinkedIn (if you use it), stick to some basic rules: good quality shot that isn't blurry, you're smiling or at least appear friendly, there isn't hair covering your eyes, and you're not wearing sunglasses. That last one is important—you've got a better chance of connecting with someone if they can see your eyes. And that great shot of you skydiving—keep it for the family album (unless it's related to your writing!).

Finally, if you'd rather people didn't see what you look like, that's absolutely fine! There's no rule that says an author has to be recognised by her readers. Elena Ferrante (author of the very successful *My Brilliant Friend*) is a perfect example of just this:

"I believe that books, once written, do not need their authors. If they have something to say, they will sooner or later find readers; if not, they won't," wrote Elena Ferrante in a 1991 letter addressed to Sandra Ozzola and Sandro Ferri, her publishers in Rome, founders of Edizioni E/O. In that letter pre-dating Ferrante's debut novel Amore Molesto (Troubling Love), published in 1992, Ferrante explained her will and determination never to reveal her true identity.

▶ https://italoamericano.org/the-mystery-of-elena-ferrante/

12

Your Publications

Readers like to know about other books and works that you've had published or are working on. Hopefully they have read one of your books, or heard about you from someone who has, and want to find out more. I'll often look up an author's website after I've finished a book, simply because I've enjoyed it and want to stay with the magic a little bit longer. If I've really enjoyed it, I might even be tempted to purchase a further book by the author.

If you have publications available to purchase, you can link to relevant sites. Try not to overcomplicate matters with too many links; just a few is fine.

Top tip: You might want to consider Universal Link (see ▶ https://books2read. com/links/ubl/create/ for more information). It's a free tool that directs readers to your book's page on their preferred retailer with just one link.

Offer Your Website Visitor Something More

If you want people to return to your website, then you need to give them an incentive. It's great that they can find out about your work, and about you, and about your upcoming events—but if you really want them to come back, you need to offer something more.

Neil Gaiman's website is a great example of this. He calls this section 'Cool Stuff & Things' which is great and is in keeping with his overall style and persona. Amongst his cool things, he offers videos, short stories, essays, audio, book excerpts, and book extras. Under his book extras he's offering pages from a notebook and sites he used for researching one of his books. That's pretty much gold dust for a fan!

Top tip: You can get creative with what you call this section—offers or extras sound pretty boring but cool stuff had me immediately clicking. Likewise, Kevin Hearne (I'll get to him shortly) calls this section Goodies!

Contact Me

People have either made the effort to find your website or come across it by chance—either way, it's an opportunity to connect and sometimes readers will want to communicate with you. Maybe they just want to share feedback or tell you how much they enjoyed your work. Other times they just want to annoy you or be unpleasant. If you don't want to open up an avenue for anyone to contact you, you certainly don't have to have a 'contact me' option on your website. But it's worth considering that we live in an online age where audiences expect to be able to reach out and contact their favourite author/celebrity/influencer. This doesn't always have to be via email—it might be tweeting a response or posting an Instagram comment, but it means they can make contact. So being that infamous author who doesn't want to be contacted might limit your readership.

While you can include your email address, this is also a way for you to end up on numerous spam lists; so if you must include an email address, I'd recommend setting up a separate one that you use specifically for your website. The better alternative is to have a 'contact me' form, which collects queries as well as email addresses without giving out your email address.

Your Blog

Blog posts are a great way to share information with your website visitors and they help to build your credibility. If you do have a blog, it should be accessible from your homepage and menu, but it should not be your homepage. A good approach is to have a link to your latest blog post on your landing homepage.

While blogs are good, remember an outdated blog doesn't create a great impression; so if you're going to include one, be committed to producing regular posts. That doesn't mean you have to post every day or even once a week. But it needs to be regular. I've just gone back to Neil Gaiman's website and I can see that he has a blog (he calls it a Journal). His last post was about 3 months ago. The one prior to that was also 3 months, so he's not exactly a prolific blog writer, but if I was a fan, I'd come to expect a post every 3 months—and actually that's not surprising when I can see all the events he has lined up over the coming months. What's important is consistency, and he seems to be offering that.

Events

This is where you can include any upcoming events such as book launches, signing, or perhaps it's an upcoming podcast about your e-book. It's where you can give interested readers details on where they can meet you, but it also shows that you're committed to your readership and keen to get out there and meet them.

I recently came across the website for author Kevin Hearne, a writer of Fantasy series. Here's his page on his events and appearances:

▶ https://kevinhearne.com/events-and-appearances/

It's a good-looking website—a great landing page that immediately drew my attention, but I really was impressed that his events' page is up to date. All too often, I come across websites with out-of-date details. The reality is, keeping information up-to-date takes time, so unless you're a big name author with a team behind you who can help, remember if you are going to include such a section, make sure you allocate time for such administration. Now, if you're an author with your first e-book and launch events are thin of the ground, you might be thinking— well this all sounds great if I actually had some events to add to a website. The trick here is to make it appear how busy you are! Share with your website visitors what you've been doing regarding your e-book. Perhaps you've been researching different publishing platforms or visited some places for research—share what you found out. Busy isn't always about public-facing events.

Do You Need to Have All These Pages?

Definitely not! I've just listed some of the typical pages you'll find but you'll find plenty of variations.

I'm going to come back to the website for Rachel Ivan (▶ http://www.rachelivan.com/). It's actually only one page but it's got the key details all there to easily find. First up is the details of her book with a short description and then where I can buy it. There's a video about the book and then finally I can sign up for her newsletter.

Capturing Email Addresses and Having Mailing Lists

Most people today are quite reluctant to hand out their email addresses—and it's not surprising when you see the volume of emails we can easily receive in a day. Therefore, it's unlikely they'll hand it over without some incentive and value to them. This is where you offer your website visitors something of value in exchange for their contact information.

What types of things can you offer as an incentive?

- An excerpt of chapter from your book
- A short story or even an entire e-book—this might seem excessive, but if you have a series, getting a reader hooked on your first book in the series, can make it worth the investment
- Something helpful—for example, some creative writing guides or worksheets

Many authors offer a mailing list. Kate Norton (author of Historical Fiction) promotes on her website that if you join her mailing list, you'll be the first to know about upcoming books, tour events, promotions, and other news. If you're a fan, that's pretty tempting!

Using Your Author Website to Market Your Books

An author website is a valuable part of your marketing strategy, but it's something that needs to be done well. Let's face it; the internet provides the online user with an endless supply of content. If our interest isn't initially sparked, then we'll move on. And let's face it, we don't want to be sold to unless it's something that we want.

This means that you need to entice the online user onto your website and for them to stay around, you need to offer them something. That something needs to be valuable to them. If you provide them with something they value—let's say they're a budding writer and they find your advice useful—then they'll come back. When it comes to an author website, an online user might seek you out because they've either read your work or heard about it, and they want to know more about you. How much you share is up to you—but it's an opportunity for them to get to know the writer you.

In saying that, the author websites that often do well are those that reflect the author's voice. If I've just finished reading a book and I've enjoyed it, I'll often go and look up their website. Things I'm interested in include other books they've written, what they might be working on, perhaps recommendations they have.

Your Authorial Voice

An author's voice and how do you reflect this in your website isn't always easy to pull off and does take some work to get it right. It includes aspects such as personality and character. When you look at the website, it immediately gives a sense of that author's personality through the design of the website, the colour choices, the images, and, of course, the text. They might write with a particular passion or humour. Perhaps there is a purpose or mission to their writing. Your voice is basically your brand—it's a style that your readers come to recognise you by.

This is the website for Om Swami: ▶ https://omswami.com/. He's been very creative with his website design, and from arriving at his homepage, it certainly grabs your interest. He's managed to create a relaxing look and feel, with aspects such as the images and with the colour tones.

Tracking Your Website's Performance

There's no point building a website and then just hoping people are seeing it. What you need is information on how many readers are finding your website and which pages are the most popular.

Google Analytics is the most in-depth and is used by more than half of all websites. It can advise you on:

- Who is visiting your website
- Where they're coming from, including their online source and geographical location
- Whether they're on a mobile or desktop device
- How many pages and which ones they visited
- How long the visits last
- Which page they visit before they exit
- How long the entire visit lasted

12

To use Google Analytics, you'll need a Google account and you can start for free.

My Final Word on Author Websites:

Be unique. While I've provided some of the more typical things you'll find on websites in this chapter, actually you need to decide what works best for you. Some of the best author websites manage to provide the information a visitor is looking for, but in unique and interesting ways. So experiment and be creative, listen to feedback, and do some research to really understand your typical readers. Then you'll have a better chance of designing a site they'll love to visit regularly.

❷ EXERCISE 12.1: Author Brands
Here are just a few authors with strong brands:
Will Smith: ▶ https://will-self.com/
Jason Reynolds: ▶ https://www.jasonwritesbooks.com/
Kate Norton: ▶ https://www.katemorton.com/
Ocean Vuong: ▶ https://www.oceanvuong.com/
Suessville: ▶ https://seussville.com

Choose two from the above (or you can also choose your favourite author/s) and see if you can identify their 'brand' in ten key words. Don't overthink this exercise, just write down six words that come to mind when you first look at their website.

For example, these are the top words that come to mind when I first go to Kate Norton's website: Professional, classical, timeless, friendly, nature, mysteries.

- **CHECKLIST: Your Author Website**

Is your upcoming e-book prominent?	While people might be interested to read an author's bio, more often than not it's their book that is the draw card. So make it the most prominent aspect of your website.
Can you easily buy your e-book from the site?	Make it as simple as possible and as obvious as possible. If your website visitor has to search for the buy me button, you need to go back to your website design drawing board.
Other publications	Can your visitors easily find these? Does the page look enticing with images of book covers? Have you included short book blurbs?
Social links	Have you linked to your other social media accounts? And can your website visitor easily find them?
Can you navigate easily to find information on the site?	Regardless of your navigation style, your visitor needs to be able to navigate more easily around without getting lost. Get someone to give it a try before you put your website live.
Is your 'About the Author' section clear and succinct?	Is it short and punchy, engaging your visitor without it feeling like a short story on your life? Does it clearly describe you as a writer? Does it create the right impression?
The type of author	If a visitor doesn't know you or your work, is it clear the type of genre or topic that you write?
Your author 'brand'	This is a tough one when you're a first-time writer, but you'll find that many successful authors have a brand that the readers can easily identify (if not perhaps describe). See if you can define your 'brand' and test your website to see if it reflects this.
Language used across your site?	Does this reflect your brand? Especially if you're a children's writer, your website is a place where you can reinforce your brand. For example, if you're a writer for children and you have a particular style, your young audience will immediately connect your books to your website, if you use the same style.
Does your personality come through?	Take a step back and consider your website as a whole? What's the image it creates? Does your personality come through? Don't just guess this—test it with others and see what they think.

Is your blog fresh and feel like it's active?	A blog isn't a necessity, but if you have one, your visitor needs to feel that it's actively being used. Do you have a schedule and ideas for upcoming posts?
Is the website design uncluttered?	If the design looks a bit like your dog's dinner—and by this I mean all over the place—then that's the impression your visitor will take away with them. Remember white space (or blank space if you have a coloured backdrop to your website) is pleasing to the eye. Too much text isn't appealing to your website visitor, so consider the overall design when reviewing a page.
Use of colour	Have you been selective in your use of colours? Just like with your e-book design, don't go overboard, and see is more when it comes to websites and colours. Once you have a colour palette you're happy with, stick to it and don't be tempted to deviate.
Are offers clear?	Are these things that your typical visitor would really want?
Are you providing your visitors with a reason to come back to your website?	Getting visitors to your website is one thing—getting them to come back is a very different prospect. If your website looks static (almost like an advertisement), there's no incentive to come back. However, if your website feels like a dynamic community where things are changing frequently, your visitors will want to pop back just in case they miss something!
Does the look and feel of your website match that of your book/s?	Consistency is good when it comes to the image you portray. So don't forget that design brief for your e-book when it comes to designing your website.
Is there a connection between your e-book and your website?	Your website should hopefully extend the world of your book for your reader. It's a place they can come to, to find out more and to linger just a little longer in the world you created for them.
Do you have a schedule in place to maintain your website?	Have a schedule and dates in your calendar so that you regularly check your website to add new content as well as updating (or removing) old content. Your website needs to grow and evolve—the writer you'll be in 12, 24, and 26 months will be very different to the one you are today. So don't forget your website—it needs to be regularly maintained.
Can your visitor reach you?	Is there a way for your website visitor to contact you?
Is your website unique?	Templates are great and very helpful with designing a website—but it can mean that websites start to look all the same and none stand out. So if you're using a template, remember to tailor it so it looks unique.

12

Managing Online Writing Projects

Contents

© The Author(s), under exclusive license to Springer Nature
Switzerland AG 2023
L. Kesteven, *Publishing Online for Writers*,
https://doi.org/10.1007/978-3-031-21366-3_13

About this Chapter

In this chapter we will:

- Consider what project management is
- Why project management is a useful skill for an author
- Cover the different stages of project management for writing projects
- EXERCISES: (1) Idea Breakdown, (2) a Plan, and (3) a Budget for Your Writing Project
- CHECKLIST: Managing online writing projects

Managing Projects or Project Management: What Is It?

Let's start with what is a project. Basically, a project is just a goal we are aiming at. For example, a project might be going on holidays, building a house, designing a computer program, or writing for an online publication. It can be as simple as making a cup of tea or as complex as designing an engine. Regardless of complexity, they all require steps to be completed in a particular order.

To achieve the goal, there will need to be a number of steps that we must go through and it's likely that these steps will need a particular order. For example, if we don't complete the step to renew our passports before we go to the airport, then we're not going to achieve our goal of going on holidays. It's also likely that we'll need to understand time frames. If we plan to renew our passports the day before we need to fly out, then we're going to be very disappointed as it will likely take a few weeks to get them arranged.

It's also possible that certain people need to perform certain tasks. If my project is building a house, I'll need to make sure that I get in the right specialists for each stage. And this is where it starts to get complicated—I need to organise the builder to construct the house before the painter arrives to do the painting. Oh no, I forgot that the electrician needs to sort out the wiring before the walls go up. You get the picture - it's all about organisation.

13

So basically project management is about:

1. INITIATION. Getting started—this is when we assess what needs to be done and clearly understanding our goal.
2. PLANNING. Identifying what needs to be done. This involves coming up with a list of activities that need to be done, finding out how long each task will take, who needs to do it, and any dependencies between activities.
3. EXECUTION. This is the actual doing stage (this might be overseeing not doing).
4. CONTROL. When it comes to projects, things will not always go according to plan. The builder will be delayed because of bad weather. COVID-19 will mean there are less staff to process passports meaning there will be delays. And the flights you booked (okay, I won't go there!). While there will be things that happen that we have no control over—such as COVID-19—we can build in contingency and stay on top of those activities we can control.
5. MANAGE. This comes down to aspects such as budget. Remember that house I mentioned earlier—we've all heard the stories of how these can too easily

exceed budgets. If we keep a close eye on our spending and know where we are exceeding what we'd planned to spend, we can make choices. We might decide to go with those expensive Italian tiles because they look amazing, but then cut back on the cabinet doors in the kitchen.

6. CLOSE. Projects have a habit of staying around for much longer than we want them to. So, it's important to officially close them so we can move onto our next project.

Time, Cost, and Quality

These are the three aspects that a project manager can work with to keep their project in control. These are: the time it needs to be complete in, a budget, and then an expected quality.

Let's say the family are planning a holiday. In terms of time, they need to travel during the school holidays, so there is no flexibility there. They also have a budget in mind—maybe they'd like to spend $2000 but are prepared to go up to $2500. But no more. Given these two factors, we have the third that we might need to be flexible with—quality. We must go at a particular time and can't spend more than $2500, so despite wanting to stay at a 4-star resort, they might need to compromise and go with a 3-star place.

I once delivered a business project where it need to be implemented before the start of the new financial year. If it wasn't on time, they wouldn't be able to invoice their customers, so there was no flexibility in terms of the delivery date. Quality was also very important - you can't have a finance system getting the figures wrong! So we certainly couldn't compromise quality. Therefore, I had to put in a lot of work upfront to ensure the costs were correctly understood—there wasn't any scope for surprises. Needless to say, this was a pretty stressful project for all the teams as we need to monitor all three aspects very closely.

My final example will be your typical building extension. I don't think I've met anyone who has had a building extension completed that delivered to schedule—often because this can be impacted by aspects outside of anyone's control. The weather is a good example of this. And often this will change with this type of project as it progresses—we think we'll spend $5000 on the floors but then we find something really nice - and before we know it the budget has been blown!

But enough talk of building houses and going on holidays, let's get back to our task at hand—that of writing for online publication.

Do Writers Have Projects?

They most definitely do! Writing this book was a project for me.

Some typical writer projects include (but not limited to):

- Researching ideas
- Writing a novel

- Getting a manuscript publication ready
- Finding an agent
- Submitting your work to an agent
- Marketing an e-book
- Self-publishing your work

This all feels very methodical. Doesn't that take the creativity out of process? Most definitely not. I consider myself to be creative—I write and enjoy designing. But I also have a project management background and before I focused on my writing, I delivered projects in the IT world. It didn't take me long to realise that—regardless of the type of project (it could be building a house, putting in a new software application, or planning an event)—everything goes more smoothly if there is some planning and management involved.

Let's face it. We're artists and very often our work doesn't always follow a structured approach. We might sudden have a great idea and then lock ourselves away to write with a mad fever. But actually, that creativity can still happen even if we apply some good project management principles. The two most definitely do not conflict and just by working with a plan doesn't need to take the creativity away. What it does mean is that it will likely make the process less stressful, leaving you more time and head space for the creativity.

The reality is, for a writer to make a living, they will need to be able to work within a budget, keep to a schedule, be expected to deliver quality work, and understand what needs to happen when. If they don't, then their budget will get blown, projects will take much longer, and delivery will be very chaotic.

Writer Projects: The Stages

13 ## Initiation

This is the initial stage where we begin to think about what we're trying to achieve or our goal.

So—why this book? Novel? Non-fiction work? Article?

Why will people want to read your work? Why are you the person to write it? Why now?

Perhaps you know of a gap in the market and your book will fill it. Perhaps you have interesting insight into a topic. Maybe you have skills or knowledge that others would find helpful. Even if you're writing a novel, it's important to consider why your idea will make a great novel that people would want to read.

Identifying your goals:

This is the outcome that you want to achieve. It might seem odd that we're starting with the end game, but if we don't understand what our goals are, then it's going to be very hard to achieve it. It's also helpful to have a clear picture of the required outcome—that way when we get to, what we hope is the end, we can test it to be sure. That means we need goals that are measurable.

A poor goal would be: I want to write a novel.

A much better goal is: I want to write a novel of 90,000 words that is a contemporary romance/comedy, and I'd like to finish it in 12 months, so that's essentially the small target of roughly 2000 words a week for 45 weeks (although there will be editing, rewrites, etc. ...).

Here's a recent example for when I wrote an article for an online magazine:

Goal: Complete an article for an online travel magazine

Length: 5000 words

Requirements: They state that they want articles suitable for a family market. Can also submit with images (with copyright permission)

Time: I want to have my article ready for their upcoming deadline (2 months away)

Sometimes it helps to break down a large activity down into multiple projects. For example, your first project might be to write your novel. The second project might be to publish your novel online. This can help you focus and with several projects, the task doesn't seem as daunting.

Scope:

This is a really important aspect, especially if you're writing a manuscript for a particular purpose. Whereas a novel can change as it develops, a piece of non-fiction needs to be more focused. Therefore, if you're writing a non-fiction book or article, you'll need to decide what is, and importantly what isn't, included. Done well, this should become your Table of Contents.

Before I started working on this book, I had the various chapters outlined. These were reviewed by others to ensure they delivered the proposed outcome of the book.

Planning

It's great to have a goal, but there's no point in starting my article for the online travel magazine, if it's going to take me 4 months to write it. Part of the process of assessing if a plan is viable, and to determine if a project is viable, you need to understand how long the activities will take.

Let's return to my article for an online travel magazine. Here are the steps I'll go through to produce this:

- Research possible article ideas (3 days)
- Produce an outline for the chosen idea (2 days)
- Write a draft (5 days)
- Find suitable photographs (2 days)
- Edit and proofread draft (2 days)
- Produce file according to magazine submission guidelines (2 days)

Now, you're probably thinking, that's all looking good. In total it will take me 16 days to produce it and I have 2 months before I need to get it in. However, I'm a freelance writer, which means that I have other writing jobs going on at the same time and I will need to fit this in around other activities, which will also need similar planning.

Break It Down

My example project is a quite small one, but if I was going to say, write a novel, then I might want to provide more detail (or sub-task) for the writing stage. For example, this might include writing character biographies, produce a high-level plot, write a chapter plan, and so on. Writing a novel is a huge undertaking—yes, some writers will just sit down and start writing, and they will take however long they take. That approach is fine if they have no time deadline they are working towards and don't mind if it takes 3 months or 3 years. Personally, I find that too daunting. I like to know that I'm making progress and to know this I break my projects down into small enough chunks.

Who Does What

For each activity, we can then identify who needs to do what. In the example above, I'm a freelancer so I completed these myself, but it's possible that you might rely on others for certain activities. Let's say I want to have someone else proofread the draft—I might need to wait until they are available. There are also relationships between the activities—for example, the person who will proofread the draft is only available in 5 days' time before they go on holidays for 10 days. Therefore, the edit and proofread activities will need to wait until this resource becomes available.

Don't think that you need to do everything yourself. If something is outside your expertise, that's okay. If your aim is to produce a professional looking e-book—if you don't have the design skills to produce your cover, it's worth the investment in getting help!

Deadlines and Dependencies

13

It's also possible that some tasks can happen without waiting for others to be completed. The activity of finding suitable photographs is a good example of this. This can happen at any time and isn't dependent on the draft being completed.

Execution

This is the stage where you deliver—for some projects this is where the house actually gets built—for a writerly project, this is where we write the book, the novel, the non-fiction article, and so on. You can give yourself an amount of time and get to work, but if you want to ensure you meet your deadline, it helps to break that into achievable chunks. For example, I like to set myself targets—for this book, I set my target at writing 2000 words a week. This included edit checking and refining the 2000 words until I was happy with it. Two-thousand words was an achievable target, and I knew that if I hit that each week, I was on track—which took the pressure off.

Stakeholders

These are the people who play an important role on your project. For example, before I started writing this book, I needed to ensure that Palgrave Macmillan was happy with my proposed Table of Contents.

Control

The only way to know if your project is in control is to capture some information. Progress is a good example - depending on the tool you're using for your writing, some will automatically tell you how many words you've written in a period or day. I use Scrivener and I find this a very helpful feature. But if you don't have this, you can always take a note of the word count when you start and check it when you've finished, then you'll know how much you've written.

Whether you edit as you go or prefer to edit at the end is very much down to the writer. Some writers prefer to get as much down on paper as they can, of their story or manuscript, and then refine and edit once they have it all down. Others prefer to write sections and then edit check it before proceeding. You'll know what works best for you. If you're in the later camp (which I am) just be careful not to spend too much time on the editing, which slows you down on getting to the next section. I allow myself a set amount of time for editing, and even if I'm not completely happy with it, I know I'll come back to it once I've completed the manuscript.

Don't Forget the Unpleasant Activities!

Yep, we all do it. These are the tasks that we'd rather not think about (and let's face it, hope would just go away!). But trust me, they won't disappear, so include them in the list and allow yourself enough time to complete them.

Manage

There are project management apps around which can help you track your progress. Even the basic free ones are fine if your project is fairly simple.

A Gantt Chart This is basically a diagram that shows your activities across a time-line. It's very visual and you can quickly see your activities and any dependencies. I like these because they quickly show me my progress, what's left to be done, and I can also see start and end dates as well any dependencies. You'll typically find a Gantt Chart produced by most project management apps or software, and they help you see how your activities are progressing—some will have progress bars where you can indicate the percentage you have completed.

But Be Warned! It's easy to get drawn into your project planning and management—remember this is to help you stay focused and keep you on track—your project plan doesn't need to look pretty and it shouldn't be taking up huge amounts of time. If you find you're spending too much time project planning and not enough time writing, stop and reassess. Maybe the app isn't what you need.

When I was delivering a conference, I was working with numerous academics, and project management wasn't their forte. That's okay—I had a list in WORD where I had the activities we need to complete, who was responsible, and the time it would take. Everyone knew what they need to do and we could tick off the activities as they got done. It was a very simple approach but it worked. So don't think you need to find a project management app and master it—it's likely that a paper to do list will work just as well.

Close

Once you've completed all the activities on your list, it's time to assess if you've achieved your goal. Remember Step 1 where we defined our goal? It's possible your goal changed as your project progressed. Maybe my article for the travel magazine morphed into something else once I did my research. That's okay; it just means that I need to change my goal to reflect what it has now become.

But it's also an opportunity to look at my requirements. I had a particular word count and it was also for a particular audience (it was a family travel site), so I need to check that I still meet these. It's possible that I found a great destination for backpackers—the idea might be a great one, but it's for a different target audience that the site I originally set out to write an article for. Therefore, I'll either have to find another magazine or have to re-work my idea.

13 Time to Reflect

Writing projects can be tough and often times were just pleased to get to the end and move on. If it wasn't a great experience, you might be eager to put it behind you and forget about it—but there might be some important lessons you can learn from the experience. Maybe you didn't allow enough time for your research, or your editing took more time than you expected. This is information that will help you next time and help you refine your project management.

Managing Multiple Projects

Where project management can really help a writer is when they are working on multiple projects at the same time. Whether you're a freelancer working for multiple clients, a student delivering assignments alongside their own writing projects, or a part-time writer who has a day job, it's likely that you're doing a lot of juggling.

It's also possible that you'll have clients asking for work to be completed by a deadline, or you submitting work to online sites that have submission windows (e.g., I recently came across an online magazine that only accepts articles twice a year in January and July). Taking on work and hoping you'll deliver to schedule isn't going to cut it—if you're delayed and miss their deadlines, it's very likely you won't get further work from them. So, time spent on some project planning and management might be a very good investment, if it can assist you in meeting schedules.

Build Your Project Activity Templates

Once you've finished a project and have the list of activities that you completed, this is a great basis for your next similar project. It's likely you'll need to refine it— no two projects are ever the same—but it's a starting point and even if the timings need to change, at least you have a list of activities to work with.

❷ EXERCISE 13.1: Idea Breakdown

What is your writerly idea?

Brainstorm your idea and jot down as many points as you can about it. You have 5 min.

For example: I want to write a magazine article of Travelling with my Dog. My notes might include: what food to bring, travel friendly pet toys, pet bedding, travelling safely with my dog in the car, where I can and can't take my dog, finding pet friendly accommodation, and so on.

Organise your idea

Take your points and see if you can group similar points together. Can you come up with a suitable heading for each group?

For example: I might combine food, pet toys, and bedding into one section called 'What to Bring'.

Do you need to do further research?

For each heading, decide if you have enough information already to write it, or do you need to do research?

For example, I need to research pet friendly accommodation further as this will depend on whether I'm writing about a specific location or a generic article.

❷ EXERCISE 13.2: A Plan

Keep it high level for the moment—you can always expand later on—but see if you can come up with ten activities you need to complete to turn your idea into a completed manuscript.

Create a table (it can be on paper, in word, or excel), and add each activity as a row:

- Who is responsible
- Time to complete
- Any activities that need to be completed before this one can start

❷ EXERCISE 13.3: A Budget

Think about your idea—are there any costs involved in producing your manuscript?

For example, I might need to visit the location for my pet article. I might need to visit a library for my research. There might be certain publications I need to purchase.

■   **CHECKLIST: Managing Online Writing Projects**

What is goal?	What do you want to achieve from this project? Be specific—define the type of form you're going to write (book, manuscript, article, journal paper, etc.)
Time	What are your time deadlines? Are these fixed or do you have some flexibility?
Cost	Do you have a budget for what you can spend on the project?
Quality	I'm not suggesting here that you write poor quality work—but think of this more as how much time you want to spend on editing and proofreading. Compromising on quality isn't worth it—but it might mean that you decide to spend some of your budget on proof reading or editing services, because you don't have the time to complete it well.
Scope	Less relevant for writers of fiction, but important for writers of non-fiction, what is in, and what is out, for your work.
Table of contents	Again, more relevant for non-fiction writers, but you should be able to produce your Table of Contents, once you know your scope.
List of activities	Produce a list of all the activities that need to be completed. Then for each one, list: • Who needs to complete it • Estimated duration
Understand dependencies	Review your activities and see if any need to be completed before others can start. For example, I can't start writing until I've completed my research.
Completed column	Add a column to your list of activities, that you can mark off when completed.
Any stakeholders	For each stakeholder, what is their role and do they need to approve any key stages or activities?
Editing approach	Will you edit as you go, or leave it until the end?
Proof reading	Who can you get to assist with this?
Lessons learnt	What have you learnt from this project that you could no better next time?

Long-Term Success for a Writer Online

Contents

© The Author(s), under exclusive license to Springer Nature Switzerland AG 2023
L. Kesteven, *Publishing Online for Writers*,
https://doi.org/10.1007/978-3-031-21366-3_14

About this Chapter

In this chapter we will consider what long-term success means for a writer when publishing online.

What do I mean by long-term success? Well for a start, success is one of those terms that can mean so many different things. And each of us will have a different idea of what success means. Someone might be happy with getting their article published by an online magazine, and once they've achieved that, their goal is to be published by further publications.

Success is going to change and evolve as we progress as writers. You might define success as getting your novel published—that's okay—but having some short-term success markers can help keep you motivated on your publishing online journey.

EXERCISES: (1) Your Writing Routine and (2) Your Writing Goals.

Won't It Be Easier to Be Published Online?

It is easier in some ways. There are many different options for getting your work published online and so many paths, such as social media and having your own blog, that publishing online makes it much easier to share your work with others. That said, with so much choice, it can be daunting. The trick is to do your groundwork first. Don't submit your work to the first site you come across—but research and make a list. Decide first your criteria for selection, and then you'll be able to assess whether a site is a good match to your needs.

But just because publications have gone online—such as magazines and journals—that doesn't mean that they have dropped their standards or are any less competitive when it comes to choosing between submissions. These online publishers will expect quality and will have a lot of people sending in their work. The reality is that you shouldn't expect that it will be an easy path, and just like any publication route, many of us will receive rejections.

Be Patient

Writing and getting published, whether online or in print, can take time. What's important is that you don't give up at the first or second or even twentieth hurdle/rejection. So long as you're getting feedback and can keep improving your writing, you're moving in the right direction. The more you keep trying, and keep writing, the better chance you have of finding success.

Selling your writing online can take time, especially if you want to sell in volumes. Even if you're working with the likes of huge online bookstores, such as Amazon, your book isn't going to sell in huge volumes immediately. In fact, I read an article recently that said the typical author took 6–9 months to build up their sales online. What's important is to monitor your sales and assess if your strategies are working as you expected. If it's not performing well, adjust your tactics.

Be Online Smart

There are scams out there, and just like any other field, there will be dodgy sites. If you're not sure whether a site is legitimate, then do some searching online about it. Generally, people online are happy to share their good and bad experiences, so if in doubt, stop and investigate. Be very careful where you send your details to and always check the terms of a site. Make sure you know what you're agreeing to—such as copyright for your work—before you send in your work.

Build on Your Writing Skills

This is what will really help your writing to standout, so spend time refining your craft. Get feedback from a range of people—readers, writers, editors, friends. It's all too easy to forget good writing habits and techniques—refresh by reading books on writing or take a course. Build your own editing checklist, so you know the usual things to check your work for. Remember that what people want online changes at a very rapid pace. There will be trends that become very popular—at the moment, the list format is popular with blog posts (e.g., the ten best places to eat out on a budget in Bali). The best way to keep up to date with trends is to be an avid online reader.

Rather like any craft—whether it's painting or cooking or building furniture—with practice we get better. And this is a huge benefit of publishing online. With different alternatives to getting work out there, we can gain experience as well as get feedback from others. I've found that writing for formats such as blog posts is hugely beneficial to my writing. This format encourages me to write regularly and succinctly. And because it's online, I can experiment with different approaches, such as the use of images.

You Need to Write

14

This one might seem like an obvious one, but unless we are dedicated to putting the time in, then our writing won't improve or our portfolio develop. If you can write every day, great—but if you can write only once a week, that's great as well. What's important is that you are consistent, and you find a space for your writing. Decide what your routine is and stick to it.

Expect Quality Writing from Yourself

Just because you can submit poor quality writing online (let's say your own blog), that doesn't mean that you should. Poorly written work can stay online for a very long time and could come back in the future to haunt you. So ensure you only submit very high quality work, regardless of the medium.

Don't Forget Your Goal

Pin it up on your wall above where you write—it will help keep you focused. It can be tempting to try something new and experiment, but if your goal is to get a novel published, then submitting short stories online is great in terms on your writing practice, but it won't help your novel progress (unless, of course, the short stories are in some way connected).

Take a Step-by-Step Approach

Publishing online can feel daunting; however, if you approach it in an organised and structured approach—following the numerous checklists I've included in this publication—then it's not difficult. It can take time but if you break it down into stages—such as completing your manuscript, getting it ready for publication, searching for suitable publishers—then it is manageable and you don't need to have extensive technical skills to complete it. Just patience and persistence (and some good project management skills! See Chap. 13).

Overnight Success Doesn't Really Happen

Sure, we've all heard the stories, but actually, go and hear some successful writers talk about their experiences. All the ones I've attended have spoken of many, many rejections before they found success. Very few writers find success happens quickly—many have written multiple novels or books before they found success.

Isn't All Publicity Good Publicity?

That isn't always the case with marketing yourself online, but I would say that when starting out, you should grab all opportunities to promote your work. Going along to that book group that only has ten members might feel like a waste of your valuable time—but if that means you have ten people who have read (and bought) your book then it's time well spent. If they enjoyed it enough to invite you to their book group then that's great. And hopefully they'll tell their friends. So, get yourself out there—look for podcasts, and other online formats that are interested in writers—approach them and offer something useful and you just might be able to give your book a quick promotion.

Learn from Others

There are many sources out there, providing useful information to other writers. I find podcasts helpful and there are a wide range of shows about writing, from finding ways through procrastination through to structured instructional sessions on writing craft. Following the Instagram, Twitter, or Facebook accounts of other writers can also provide you with a range of tips as well as understanding how writers' day-to-day lives can differ greatly. All writers are learning and adapting to new trends or formats.

Build Up Your Network

If people know, like, and trust you, they'll want to work with you. That applies whether it's another business, other writers, or your customers and followers. Building up trust takes time and relationships are formed through an exchange that is mutually beneficial to both parties. People will buy your book because they want to read it, but they will only join your email list if they feel there is something of value to them. Think about what value you could provide them. Deliver that and you're on your way to having success with publishing online.

Brace Yourself for Feedback

Generally speaking, there are writers and readers out there who are happy to provide helpful and constructive feedback. You just need to find them. Don't expect that you'll always receive reasonable feedback—sadly, there are people out there who you'd rather not meet. It's important to understand that for, whatever reason, not all feedback will be reasonable, fair, or even nice. There is one benefit to receiving feedback online—you don't have to meet the reviewer in person, and you can delete it and block them. So, if it gets nasty, don't be tempted to respond and tell them how wrong they are, simply walk away. It's very unlikely they will engage in any rational conversation. We are not going to please all of the people all of the time and equally not all the people we try to like are going to like us back.

14

Enjoy the Process of Writing

Writing is a tough business and it involves rejections (often a lot of them)—remember J. K. Rowling was rejected by just about everyone and the first Harry Potter book was on its last legs. And it's much easier to say—take them on the chin and move on—than it is in reality. Rejections are hard. They knock us down and often it feels like all our hard work has been for nothing. The only advice I can give is to find a circle of writer friends that you can turn to. They are the only ones that truly understand how upsetting it is and support you to move on.

So rather than focusing on the end goal, try to enjoy the process of writing itself. Let's face it, finding success is tough so why not find pleasure in the process rather than the end goal.

Don't Give Up

Many writers give up too soon. They expect to have readers to love their work right away, and when that doesn't happen, they throw their manuscript onto the fire. If you publish a novel online, it can feel disheartening when you finally see your work online at Amazon, and then no one is purchasing it. This is where you need to take a step back and accept that your work won't sell itself. If it's not selling then your marketing strategy isn't working; it may not be to do with the quality of your work. And if you don't have a marketing strategy then that's your answer.

Don't Be Afraid of Experimentation

The great thing about publishing online is that you can give things a try. If they don't work or you don't enjoy it, then you can adapt or try something else. Just because you haven't written a blog post doesn't mean that you can't give it a shot. With some online formats, the threshold is lower to get your work out there.

If you've always published in one particular journal, expand your reach and see if others might be interested. The one thing about the online world is that it is massive—so incomprehensibly large and with such a multitude of options. In the past, writers needed to find someone who believed in their work, to get published. That's changed and with publishing online, the writer can be in the driving seat, making decisions about their writing career.

And if something isn't working, investigate options. For example, if your book isn't selling, investigate why this might be. Are enough people finding out about it? Are there marketing channels that you haven't considered yet. Get advice from others and see what has worked for them. It's all too easy to assume it's the book's fault that it isn't selling but it's very possible that it's sitting on that metaphorical online 'top shelf right at the back' and no-one can actually find it!

Take a Break If You Need To

If it feels like you're continuing to hit your head into a brick wall then it's time to take a breather. It's all good and well for me to advise to brush yourself off and get back up again, but the reality is that rejection is hard to deal with. Sometimes you just need space and time. I've been there—I've had some rejections that were very hard to stomach—so I put the emails into a folder and didn't come back to them until after a period of time. That first moment when you receive a rejection is a shock—but once you've given it time, you'll come back and see that maybe they had some useful advice. Maybe they didn't! In which case, it's their loss! But a break can refresh you and give you a fresh start to look at your project through your experienced eyes.

Don't Go It Alone

Learn from others and build up a network of like-minded writers who are publishing online. It's an opportunity to share your experiences as well as giving each other support. The web has opened up the world for writers, giving us access to other sites, to other writers, and to other readers. Take advantage of this and expand your reach.

Brush Up on the Marketing Skills

Even the best-written work won't find an online audience if it isn't marketed well. Sure, someone might stumble across it and tell their friends, but that's a pretty small market. Just because you're a writer, that doesn't preclude you from also becoming a good marketeer. There are plenty of resources online—just like my advice above on finding writing advice online—start with podcasts.

Branding

Consistency is important, and if you want to portray yourself as a particular type of author, then your brand needs to come through in all aspects of your marketing. Whether that's when readers visit your website, or when they meet you at a book signing. Consider your style, your writing style, your image.

14   Always Be Professional

Sure, there are plenty of people online who aren't professional, but you'll do yourself no favours if you drop your standards. Avoid getting involved in online spats—even if you've got a valid point, these things can very quickly escalate and get out of hand. Your online legacy isn't easily removed, so be careful about what you leave behind. When dealing with anyone online, remember that they want to work with people who are easy to deal with and won't make their life difficult. So be polite and show them you're a delight to work with!

Watch Your Writing Online

Unfortunately for writers, on a daily basis, our craft is on show for all to see. If we write Twitter posts that are full of grammatical errors, then readers will rightly question our ability to produce quality text. So every little bit of writing you put out there—even the small comment—is a demonstration of your writing talent.

Be Prepared

The world is changing at a very fast pace, whether that's with the technology we as writers use, the topics people are interested in, the formats available to us. Who could have anticipated in the early 2000s, how popular Twitter would become (launched in 2006) or how the short format post would take off. Therefore, being prepared and being adaptable are important skills. Take for example Kindle and its recent move away from MOBI files, requiring writers to change the files they produce. Even the world of online reading is changing—and the technology moves on every year. Such as with photographers and their world going digital, so to do writers need to accommodate and move forward. To anticipate what the future might hold, step outside of yourself and consider the bigger picture. If you can understand trends and what's happening in the world in general, you might be able to take a view where your own field is heading.

Diversify

Don't put all your eggs in one basket, as the saying goes; it is very important when it comes to publishing online, especially if you want to make a living. Sites can come and go very quickly, and while you might be very happy with your ongoing contract to write for a publisher on a regular basis, that could quickly change. So, the more revenue streams you have—though of course, it needs to be manageable— the less you'll be hit if one of them drops out.

Ask for Help

If you don't know how to do something, then reach out. There are resources available online and other writers who have probably shared your experience. Finding other like-minded writers is invaluable—if you don't know where to start, then explore online groups on platforms such as Facebook.

Should You Consider a Self-Publishing Company?

These are companies that help authors self-publish books. They can assist you through the process of publishing online, how to use technology, and by providing services, such as editing. These companies are generally profit-making, and depending on the service/s offered, will charge a fee. It's useful to shop around because what they charge can vary. Remember too, it's in their interest to get your business, so they will, more than likely, give your work praise and positive feedback. That's not to say they shouldn't, but you need to be knowledgeable that their business model is based on assisting authors who want to get published.

There are three main types of self-publishing companies:
1. publishing platforms (e.g., Amazon)
2. author services (e.g., Reedsy)
3. self-publishing education companies (they will assist you through the self-publishing process)

My advice would be to outsource those parts of the process you're not comfortable doing yourself. For example, you might want to get someone to draw the images for your children's picture book. That said, some people have told me that using a self-publishing company was a great way to learn.

When publishing online, the writer is in the driving seat, which is great when it comes to making decisions. However, it also has the downside in that you don't have that support base around you. You won't have your agent calling you regularly to remind you that you have a deadline looming. You won't have a marketing team to advise you on the best cover to suit the current market. And you won't have a sales team advising you to do more promotional work. Therefore, you'll need to push yourself!

❷ EXERCISE 14.1: Your Writing Routine

Let's think about our writing and design a routine that will work for us (that means it will fit in with everything else that we do). If you work full-time and have a family, while you might want to write on the weekends, that simply might not be possible. Instead, focus on what's achievable.

14

How much time (in hours) can you set aside for your writing each week?	
What day/s work best?	
Is there a time of day that is easier?	
Do you have a place which is your writing area (you might be lucky enough to have a dedicated study, others might make a dedicated desk)?	
If you share your home, how will others know that you're writing and not interrupt you?	

? EXERCISE 14.2: Your Writing Goals

Goals are important and help us keep focused. Especially when we're online, there are plenty of distractions—yes, we've all been there—browsing the web when we should be writing. Knowing our goal/s and reminding us of these can help us achieve them.

What do you want to achieve with your writing?	
In the next month?	
In the next 3 months?	
In the next year?	
Do you need to do anything to help you get there (aside from the time)—for example, help, skills, training?	

Supplementary Information

Index